How to Cook
for People with Diabetes

How to Cook
for People with Diabetes

American
Diabetes
Association®

Book Acquisitions	Susan Reynolds
Book Editor	Laurie Guffey
Contributing Editor	Karen Lombardi Ingle
Production Director	Carolyn R. Segree
Production Coordinator	Peggy M. Rote

Page design and typesetting services by Insight Graphics
Cover design by Wickham & Associates, Inc.
Cover photography by Aldo Tutino
Illustrations by Rebecca Grace Jones

Printed in the United States of America

American Diabetes Association
1701 N. Beauregard Street
Alexandria, VA 22311

Library of Congress Cataloging-in-Publication Data
How to cook for people with diabetes / American Diabetes Association.
    p.   cm.
   Includes index.
   ISBN 0-945448-68-6 (pb)
   1. Diabetes--Diet therapy--Recipes.   I. American Diabetes
Association.
RC662.H685 1996
641.5'6314--dc21

96-48837
CIP

Editorial Advisory Board

Wylie McNabb, EdD
The University of Chicago Center for Medical
    Education and Health Care
Chicago, Illinois

Virginia Peragallo-Dittko, RN, MA, CDE
Winthrop University Hospital
Mineola, New York

Jacqueline Siegel, RN
St. Joseph Hospital
Seattle, Washington

Tim Wysocki, PhD
Nemours Children's Center
Jacksonville, Florida

Contents

Foreword

During the course of my usual clinic day, I have many opportunities to discuss the treatment of diabetes with patients, family members, and health care providers. I always hesitate to use the word "diet" in these discussions because of the immediate association with deprivation—not being able to include the foods you love to eat in your meal plan. This negative connotation is a major barrier in achieving the positive behavioral changes that are the key to managing diabetes.

However, as this latest book of recipes from the American Diabetes Association (ADA) demonstrates, there are many ways to include many of your favorite foods in a well-balanced meal plan. In *Diabetes Forecast*, the ADA's monthly magazine on healthy living with diabetes, we have tried to help people recognize that there is no "ideal diet" or universal "best diet" for people with diabetes. Instead, through our great-tasting recipes and accurate nutritional information, we try to encourage people to meet their individual needs through a variety of creative, tasty food solutions. You'll find the best of these recipes in this book.

Certainly, people with diabetes first need to acquire a basic, well-rounded knowledge base in nutrition. Then, by trying different foods and measuring blood sugar levels before and after meals, people can learn what works best for them. This is what successful, individualized diabetes self-management is all about. In the press, the dietary debate concerning the best balance between carbohydrates, protein, and fat will no doubt continue. The recipes in this book try to strike a reasonable balance between these philosophies to produce dishes that not only taste great, but comply with well-established nutritional guidelines.

If you're tired of preparing the same old meals, try the ethnic American and international recipes in "Recipes from around the World." Liven up your holidays with a "New-Fashioned Thanksgiving" or a "Fabulous Fourth." Learn how to make pasta, cook with parchment, and prepare delicious gifts to give to friends and family.

I have always looked forward to the recipes in each new issue of *Diabetes Forecast* so my appetite could be pleasantly stimulated. I hope all of you, with or without diabetes, will enjoy the recipes as much as the people who created them.

Neal Friedman, MD
Editor-in-Chief, *Diabetes Forecast*

Acknowledgments

The American Diabetes Association is grateful to the following individuals who contributed to this book: Connie Crawley, MS, RD, LD, and Carolyn Leontos, MS, RD, CDE, who reviewed the introductory material; Madelyn Wheeler, MS, RD, CDE, of Nutritional Computing Concepts, Inc., who reviewed the nutrient analyses; and Marcia Mazur, Senior Editor of *Diabetes Forecast*, who has worked diligently for many years to bring healthy, delicious recipes to her readers.

Portions of this book were drawn from the following articles that originally appeared in *Diabetes Forecast*. Because some recipes predate current food labeling practices, in some cases not all nutrient information is provided. If a given value is not present, it would not be accurate to assume the value is zero. The Association appreciates the contribution of the original article authors.

"Dinner Is in the Bag," Marcia Levine Mazur, May 1995
"Add Verve with Herbs," Joyce P. Barnett, March 1994
"The World's Greatest Pasta: Yours!" Mary M. Austin, September 1994
"Mixing Up Magic," Nadine Uplinger, September 1993
"The Pressure Is On," Carolyn Leontos and Laura Asgarian, September 1992
"The Grill of a Lifetime," Harold Holler, May 1991
"Treating Leftovers Right," Sue McLaughlin, November 1991
"Cooking for You," Debra Schmidt, May 1990
"With Love from You," Marcia Ferguson and Karmeen Kulkarni, November 1990
"Goulash by Gosh," Elsa Ramirez Brisson, April 1995
"Presents from the Past," E. Barrie Kavasch, January 1994
"Persia on a Platter," Mehrnaz Sajedi, May 1994
"Foods from the Heart of Germany," Joyce P. Barnett, January 1993

Introduction

How to Cook for People with Diabetes

Cooking for a person with diabetes means cooking in healthful ways. Healthful cooking is choosing and preparing foods so that they are low in saturated fat and cholesterol, moderate in salt and sugars, and high in starches and fiber.

Making healthful changes in the way you prepare food is important, but so is choosing the healthiest foods at the grocery store. This introduction provides information on cooking techniques; suggestions for cooking with less fat, sodium, and cholesterol; ways to increase fiber and complex carbohydrates in your diet; and guidelines for choosing the best foods at the grocery store. Use these ideas when you prepare the recipes in this book and in your everyday life.

Cooking Lingo

Whether you are just learning to cook or have been cooking for a long time, this list of the cooking terms referred to in the recipes in this book, plus a few others, will get you started on your way to cooking for people with diabetes.

Dry Heat Cooking Methods

There are two main ways to cook food: with dry heat or moist heat. Dry heat cooking methods use hot air to cook food and often require the addition of some fat, such as oil, butter, or margarine. Dry heat cooking methods include:

Baking: cooking food in an oven.
Roasting: cooking food, usually meats or poultry, in an uncovered pan in an oven.

Broiling: cooking food directly under or over a heat source, such as under the broiler in an oven or on top of a barbecue grill.

Pan-broiling: cooking meats or fish quickly over high heat in a heavy pan, with little or no fat. Fat drippings from the food are poured off as they form.

Grilling: cooking food over a heat source on a gas, charcoal, or electric grill.

Browning: cooking food quickly over high heat, causing the outside of the food to turn brown while the inside stays moist. Browning can be done on top of a stove or under the broiler in an oven.

Sauteing: cooking thin or minced food quickly in a small amount of hot fat over direct heat in an open pan, which is kept in motion.

Pan-frying: cooking food in a moderate amount of hot fat over direct heat in an open pan.

Stir-frying: cooking small pieces of food quickly in a small amount of hot fat over very high heat in a large open pan, while constantly and briskly stirring the food.

Deep-frying: cooking food in hot fat that is deep enough to cover the food.

Even though most of these cooking methods use hot fat, many can be modified so that less fat is used (see *Cooking Techniques to Lower Fat*). The only cooking method to avoid is deep-frying, because of the large amount of fat needed.

Moist Heat Cooking Methods
Moist heat cooking methods use a hot liquid or very moist hot air to cook food. Moist heat cooking methods use very little or no fat. Moist heat cooking methods include:

Boiling: cooking food in a liquid that has been heated to 212°F at sea level. A liquid is boiling when large bubbles form and break on the surface.

Parboiling: partially cooking food by boiling it briefly.

Double-boiling: cooking food over a boiling liquid. It is usually done with two pots, one sitting partially inside the other. The lower pot holds the liquid, while the upper pot holds the food.

Poaching: cooking food in a liquid at or just below the boiling point. The amount of liquid varies, but does not cover the food.

Simmering: cooking food in a liquid that has been heated to between 140 and 185°F at sea level. A liquid is simmering when tiny bubbles come to the surface and barely seem to break.

Stewing: barely covering food with a liquid and simmering slowly for a long time in a tightly covered pot.

Steaming: cooking food on a rack or in a steamer basket over boiling or simmering water in a covered pan.

Blanching: heating food, then rapidly cooling it. Blanching can be done by putting food into boiling water and then into cold water, or by steaming food and then refrigerating it.

Braising: browning food, then cooking it in a small amount of liquid at low heat for a long time, while keeping it tightly covered. Braising can be done on top of a stove or in an oven.

Other Cooking Terms

Dredge: to lightly coat food with flour, cornmeal, or bread crumbs, such as before frying.

Dutch oven: a large pot or kettle with a tight-fitting lid used for moist heat cooking methods, such as braising and stewing.

Marinate: to soak a food in a seasoned liquid mixture.

Microwave: to cook, heat, or defrost food in a microwave oven.

Pressure cooker: a cooking pot with an airtight lid and valve system that regulates pressure. Foods get cooked at high temperatures as the pressure cooker builds up steam.

Puree: to grind or mash food until it is completely smooth. Pureeing can be done using a food processor, blender, or sieve.

Cooking with Less Fat and Cholesterol

The two main kinds of fat in food are saturated fat and unsaturated fat. Saturated fat is highest in animal foods and some plant foods. However, most plant foods are high in unsaturated fat. Unsaturated fat can be mostly polyunsaturated or monounsaturated. Cholesterol is found only in animal foods.

Foods that tend to be high in saturated fat and/or cholesterol are whole-milk dairy products, fatty cuts of meat, and certain oils and salad dressings. Here are some tips for choosing lower-fat versions of these foods at the grocery store, followed by cooking techniques to lower fat and ways to make recipes lower in fat.

Choosing Foods Lowest in Fat
Cheese: Look for low-fat, reduced-fat, or fat-free cheeses. Choose those with 5 to 6 grams of fat per 1-ounce serving or less. Try part-skim and fat-free mozzarella, nonfat or low-fat ricotta, farmer cheese, and nonfat or low-fat cottage cheese.

Fish and shellfish: Most fish and shellfish are naturally low in calories. Most also have less saturated fat and cholesterol than meats. Choose unbreaded plain fresh or frozen fish and canned fish packed in water. Or rinse oil-packed fish under running water to remove the added vegetable oil.

Meats: Buy lean cuts of meat. Avoid cured or smoked meats, including hot dogs, salami, bologna, bacon, and sausage.

4

These tend to be higher in fat. Look for lunch meats with 3 grams or less of fat per ounce. Consider game meats, like venison and rabbit. They tend to be leaner than other meats.

Top 5 Leanest Cuts of Meats

Beef	Lamb	Pork	Veal
Top round	Foreshank	Tenderloin	Leg
Eye round	Shank	Sirloin chop	Arm roast
Shank crosscuts	Leg	Loin roast	Sirloin
Tip round	Sirloin	Top loin chop	Blade roast
Bottom round	Arm roast	Loin chop	Loin

Milk and cream: Choose skim milk, 1% milk, or buttermilk made from skim milk instead of whole or 2% milk. Substitute nonfat dry milk or evaporated skim milk for cream or half-and-half. Be wary of powdered nondairy creamers made with palm or coconut oils, which are high in saturated fat. Choose a liquid nondairy creamer made with unsaturated oils.

Oils: Choose polyunsaturated vegetable oils, such as corn, cottonseed, safflower, sesame, soybean, and sunflower. And choose monounsaturated oils, such as olive, avocado, almond, canola, and peanut. Choose tub, liquid, light, or diet margarine that is labeled low in trans fatty acids.

Poultry: White meat is less fatty than dark meat. Boneless, skinless chicken and turkey breasts are the leanest. When buying ground chicken or turkey, look for those labeled as having less than 7 to 8% fat by weight (36% or less of its calories from fat).

Salad dressings: Look for reduced-calorie or fat-free salad dressings with less than 20 to 30 calories and about 5 grams of fat per 2 tablespoons. Dilute regular salad dressings with fat-free ones. Or use half a serving (1 tablespoon) of a regular salad dressing. Look for fat-free or reduced-fat mayonnaise with 5 grams of fat per tablespoon. Try flavored vinegars.

Yogurt: Choose low-fat or nonfat yogurt instead of whole-milk yogurt.

Cooking Techniques to Lower Fat
One way to cook with less fat is to change your cooking technique. Here are some cooking techniques to lower fat.

■ Select nonstick cookware. With nonstick cookware, you won't need to use as much fat. Often, you won't need to use any fat, especially if you start cooking at a low temperature.

■ Saute or stir-fry with a tablespoon or less of an unsaturated oil.

■ Saute or stir-fry with nonstick vegetable oil spray, wine, or nonfat or low-fat broth instead of oil.

■ Top baked potatoes, air-popped popcorn, or roast turkey or chicken with butter-flavored nonstick cooking spray instead of butter or margarine.

■ Microwave onions, garlic, peppers, and other vegetables in a bit of water instead of sauteing them in oil.

■ Trim fat from meat either before or after cooking.

■ Take skin off poultry after cooking.

■ Brown meat in a nonstick pan with little or no oil.

■ Avoid deep-frying, pan-frying, or sauteing in lots of oil or other fats.

- Roast, grill, or broil on a rack so the fat drains off and away from the food.

- Drain the fat as it cooks out when pan-frying.

- Baste with broth, vegetable or fruit juice, or wine rather than with pan drippings.

- Marinate meats and vegetables in lemon juice, lime juice, sherry, wine, vinegar, low-fat or nonfat broth, or vegetable juice instead of oil. Marinate in herbs and spices, which add flavor with little or no fat or calories.

- Skim the fat from soups, stews, broths, gravies, and sauces. Chilling the food in the refrigerator until the fat floats on top and hardens makes the fat easier to remove.

Making Recipes Lower in Fat

Another way to cook with less fat is to substitute a lower-fat ingredient for a higher-fat one in a recipe. Here's a list of sample ingredients and healthier substitutes for cooking and baking.

Ingredient	Substitute
Butter (for baking)	Butter and applesauce or other mashed fruit (1 to 1 or 3/4 to 1/4)
Butter (for cooking)	Butter and vegetable oil whipped together (1 to 1) or oil alone (1/4 to 1/3 less)
Cheese	Low-fat or nonfat cheese, or use less of a sharper regular cheese
Chocolate	Cocoa and vegetable oil (3 to 1) or cocoa and strained prunes (enough to moisten)
Cream, heavy	Evaporated skim milk or skim milk and vegetable oil (2 to 1)

Ingredient	Substitute
Cream, light	Skim milk and evaporated skim milk (1 to 1)
Cream cheese	Low-fat or fat-free cream cheese, Neufchatel, pureed low-fat cottage cheese, or yogurt cheese
Evaporated milk	Evaporated skim milk
Frosting	Sifted powdered sugar
Half-and-half	Evaporated skim milk
Margarine (for baking)	Margarine and applesauce or other mashed fruit (1 to 1 or 3/4 to 1/4)
Margarine (for cooking)	Margarine and bouillon (1 to 3)
Mayonnaise	Plain low-fat or nonfat yogurt and mayonnaise (1 cup to 1 Tbsp) or reduced-calorie or fat-free mayonnaise
Nuts	Grape-nuts®, low-fat granola cereal, bran cereal (All-Bran®, 100% Bran®)
Oil (for baking)	Oil and applesauce or other mashed fruit (1 to 1 or 2 to 1)
Oil (for cooking)	Oil and bouillon (1 to 1) or non-stick cooking spray
Shortening (for baking)	Shortening and applesauce or other mashed fruit (1 to 1 or 3/4 to 1/4)
Shortening (for cooking)	Vegetable oil (1/4 to 1/3 less)
Sour cream	Plain low-fat or nonfat yogurt, pureed low-fat cottage cheese with a little lemon juice, light or nonfat sour cream, or yogurt cheese
Whipped cream	Whipped evaporated skim milk
Whole egg	2 egg whites or egg substitute
Whole milk	Skim or 1% milk, evaporated skim milk, or nonfat dry milk

Cooking with More Starches and Fiber

Starches are one of the two major types of carbohydrate. The other major type is sugar (see below). Starches include breads, cereals, pasta, rice, potatoes, corn, dry beans, and peas. Most starches have very little fat or cholesterol. Starches that tend to be high in fat, such as biscuits, croissants, some muffins, and corn bread, are best avoided.

Fiber is the part of plants that your body can't digest. Fiber is found in fruits, vegetables, legumes (beans, peas, and lentils), and whole grains. All are low in fat and calories and have no cholesterol. Try these suggestions for choosing and using starches and fiber.

Choosing Breads
For the most fiber, go for breads that list whole grains or multigrains as the first ingredient on the label. Whole-grain breads include whole wheat, oatmeal, rye, and pumpernickel. Look for those with 2 to 3 grams of fiber per slice.

Choosing Cereals
Look for a breakfast cereal that has

■ No more than 2 grams of fat per serving.

■ No more than 6 grams of sugars per serving.

■ Less than 150 calories per serving.

■ Less than 400 grams of sodium per serving.

■ At least 4 grams of fiber per serving.

Using Cereals

■ Sprinkle a high-fiber dry cereal over plain or flavored nonfat yogurt or nonfat frozen yogurt.

■ Add high-fiber dry cereal to breads, hot cereals, casseroles, and stuffings.

Choosing Fruits

Choose fresh, frozen (without added sugar), canned (in water or juice), or dried fruit. If you buy canned fruit packed in syrup, rinse the syrup off under cold water. Limit dried fruits to a 1/4-cup serving. When choosing fresh fruits, follow these guidelines:

Apples: Look for apples that are firm and well colored, with a fresh fragrance and no bruises. Refrigerate.

Apricots: Look for apricots that are plump and somewhat firm, with smooth skin and a uniform color (not green). Ripen at room temperature until apricots feel soft; refrigerate.

Bananas: Look for bananas with even-colored yellow skin, with or without brown specks. Store at room temperature until ripe, then refrigerate. The skin will turn black, but the inside will be fine.

Blackberries: Look for blackberries that are plump, firm, and deep colored, with no hulls or mold. Refrigerate, unwashed and uncovered.

Blueberries: Look for blueberries that are plump, firm, and dry, with a frosted purple-blue color. Refrigerate, unwashed and uncovered.

Cantaloupe: Look for a cantaloupe that is firm, unbruised, and heavy for its size, with a thick, well-raised, yellowish (not green) netting and sweet aroma. Ripen at room temperature. Refrigerate when ripe.

Cherries: Look for cherries that are plump, firm, brightly colored, and glossy, with pliable stems attached. Refrigerate, unwashed and uncovered.

Currants: Look for currants that are firm and plump, without hulls. Refrigerate, unwashed and uncovered.

Grapes: Look for grapes that are plump, full colored, and firmly attached to their stems. Refrigerate, unwashed.

Grapefruit: Look for grapefruit that are firm, heavy for their size, and springy (not spongy) when pressed, with thin smooth skin. Refrigerate.

Honeydew: Look for a honeydew that is heavy for its size, with a velvety and somewhat sticky skin. Ripen at room temperature. Refrigerate when ripe.

Kiwis: Look for kiwis that are slightly soft to firm, with no soft spots or bruises. Refrigerate.

Lemons: Look for lemons that are firm, plump, and heavy for their size, with smooth, brightly colored yellow skin (no tinge of green). Refrigerate.

Limes: Look for limes that are firm, plump, and heavy for their size, with smooth, brightly colored green skin (small brown areas on skin are okay). Refrigerate.

Mangoes: Look for mangoes that are fragrant and yield to gentle pressure, with unblemished, mostly yellow-to-red skin. Unripe mangoes are green. Ripen at room temperature in a paper bag. Refrigerate when ripe.

Oranges: Look for oranges that are firm, heavy for their size, and slightly shiny, with smooth skin that is free of mold or spongy spots. Refrigerate or leave at a cool room temperature.

Papayas: Look for papayas that are mostly yellow. Ripen at room temperature until they turn golden and yield slightly to pressure. Refrigerate when ripe.

Peaches: Look for peaches that are intensely fragrant and that yield to gentle pressure. Ripen at room temperature. Refrigerate when ripe.

Pears: Look for pears that are fragrant and free of soft spots. Ripen at room temperature. Pears ripen from the inside out. They are ripe when the neck yields to pressure. They are overripe when soft on the outside. Refrigerate when ripe.

Pineapples: Look for pineapples that are firm or slightly soft, full colored, with no greening, and sweet smelling at the base. Pineapples won't ripen after picking, but turn them upside down a day or so before eating so the sweet juices at the top run down to the base. Refrigerate.

Pomegranates: Look for pomegranates that are heavy for their size, richly colored, and free of blemishes. Refrigerate or store in cool, dry place.

Raspberries: Look for raspberries that are plump, brightly colored, and dry and cool, without hulls or mold. Refrigerate, unwashed and uncovered.

Strawberries: Look for strawberries that are plump, firm, dry, shiny, and fully colored, with a green cap stem attached. Refrigerate, unwashed.

Watermelon: Look for a whole watermelon that makes a ping or high-pitched thud when you knock on it. Look for a watermelon section that is tight, dark red, and moist looking. Store uncut watermelon in a cool, dark place. Refrigerate cut sections.

Using Fruits

■ Add blueberries, peaches, or bananas to cold cereal.

■ Add raisins or pieces of dried apricots or apples to hot cereal.

■ Put a few raisins, dates, pieces of apple or dried apricot, or pineapple chunks on a salad.

■ Toss fruit into entrees. Try pineapple in a stir-fry or on pizza, fresh or dried cranberries or peaches in chicken dishes, or apricots or apples in pork dishes.

■ Leave skins on apples, peaches, and other fruits.

■ Add dried apricots, apples, or pears to plain or flavored nonfat yogurt or nonfat frozen yogurt.

Choosing Grains

Look for grains that are even in size and color. Fresh grains smell nutty, not musty or moldy. Store grains in tightly covered jars in the refrigerator. If you are not able to find a particular grain in your local supermarket, try a health-food store or ethnic market. Here's a list of grains used in the recipes in this book.

Barley: comes in three notable types: hulled, Scotch, and pearled. Hulled barley has had only the outer husk removed. Scotch barley has been husked and coarsely ground. Pearled barley has been husked, has had the bran removed, and has been steamed and polished.

Bran: the outer layer of a grain. Examples are corn bran, oat bran, rice bran, and wheat bran.

Buckwheat: an herb, not a grain. Its tiny seeds are used to make buckwheat flour. Buckwheat seeds that have been hulled and crushed are called grouts. Cooked or roasted grouts are called kasha.

Bulgur: wheat kernels that have been parboiled, dried, and broken up.

Cornmeal: dried, ground corn kernels. Cornmeal is yellow, white, or blue, depending on the type of corn used.

Couscous: hard-cracked granules of semolina.

Grouts: hulled, crushed grain, such as barley, buckwheat, or oats.

Hominy: dried white or yellow corn kernels from which the hull and germ have been removed.

Oats: hulled and toasted oats are called oat grouts. Oat grouts that have been steamed and rolled flat are known as old-fashioned oatmeal or rolled oats.

Rice: brown rice has had the outer husk and a small portion of the bran removed. White rice has had the husk, bran, and germ removed. Rice comes in many varieties. Some varieties include Indian basmati, American texmati, Italian arborio, and Japanese mochi.

Semolina: coarsely ground durum wheat.

Wheat: comes in three major types: hard wheat, soft wheat, and durum wheat. The wheat kernel is made up of bran, germ, and endosperm.

Wheat germ: the embryo of the wheat kernel.

Wild rice: the whole seed of a marsh grass native to America.

Using Grains

- Add wheat germ to breads, hot cereals, casseroles, and stuffings.

- Use brown rice instead of white rice.

- Toss brown rice, bulgur, or another cooked grain into soups, stews, salads, or casseroles.

- Replace some of the meat in meat loaf or meatballs with bulgur, brown rice, or another cooked grain.

- Replace some all-purpose flour with whole-wheat flour when baking. Start with a quarter of the total amount of flour. Move to half a cup of white flour and half a cup of whole-wheat flour for each cup of flour needed.

Choosing Legumes

Buy dried beans and lentils, fresh or frozen peas, and canned beans without added salt. Choose fat-free varieties of refried beans, baked beans, and vegetarian chili. When buying dried beans, look for a smooth skin without cracks. Store in a moisture-proof container or bag. Dried beans will endure most temperatures. Use them within a year. You'll find some of these beans used in the recipes in this book.

Black bean: black skin, cream-colored flesh, sweet flavor.

Black-eyed pea: beige with a black circle on skin.

Chickpea: round, buff colored, nutty flavor. Also called garbanzo bean.

Green bean: long slender green pods with small seeds inside. Pod and seeds are edible. Also called string bean and snap bean.

Green pea: round and green. Pod is not edible. Also called garden pea or English pea.

Kidney bean: reddish-brown skin, cream-colored flesh.

Lentil: tiny, lens shaped, with a grayish brown outside and creamy yellow inside. There is also a red variety.

Lima bean: light green skin, cream-colored flesh.

Navy bean: small and white. Also known as a Yankee bean.

Snow pea: bright green pod with tiny seeds inside. Pod and seeds are edible.

Split pea: a green or yellow field pea that has been dried.

Wax bean: a pale yellow variety of the green bean.

Using Legumes

- Add about 1/4 cup of cooked beans, peas, or lentils to soups, stews, and casseroles.

- Top your salads with peas, chickpeas, or green beans.

- Top rice, pasta, or couscous with cooked black beans, kidney beans, or lentils.

- Use legumes in place of ground meat in recipes. Try kidney beans in tomato sauce, meat loaf, or lasagna.

Choosing Pasta

For the least fat, choose pasta made without eggs or oil.

Try fiber-rich, whole-wheat pasta and low-cholesterol, yolk-free pasta. Dry pasta is less expensive and stores longer than fresh.

Choosing Vegetables

Choose plain fresh, frozen, or canned vegetables. Avoid vegetables in cream sauces, butter, or margarine. When buying fresh vegetables, follow these guidelines:

Alfalfa sprouts: Look for alfalfa sprouts that are crisp and tender, with little or no liquid at the bottom of the container. Refrigerate.

Artichokes: Look for artichokes that are plump, heavy for their size, and compact, with tightly closed leaves. Fresh artichokes will squeak when rubbed against each other. Refrigerate.

Beet greens: Look for beet greens that are crisp and bright green, not yellowed. Refrigerate.

Beets: Look for beets that are firm, with smooth skins and some greens still attached. Refrigerate, unwashed.

Bell peppers: Look for bell peppers that are firm, glossy, bright colored, and free of spots or bruises. Refrigerate.

Bok choy: Look for bok choy that has tender dark green leaves and crisp white stalks. Refrigerate.

Broccoli: Look for broccoli that has firm stalks and compact green or purplish green buds, free of yellowing. Refrigerate, unwashed.

Brussels sprouts: Look for Brussels sprouts that have a clean, white core and bright green, compact heads that are heavy for their size. Refrigerate, unwashed.

Cabbage: Look for a cabbage that is firm, heavy for its size, and compact, with crisp leaves. Refrigerate.

Carrots: Look for carrots that are firm and smooth, with moist bright greens, if attached. Refrigerate.

Cauliflower: Look for a cauliflower that is firm and compact, without spots or bruises. Refrigerate, unwashed.

Celeriac: Look for celeriac that is firm and small, with hard roots and no soft spots. Refrigerate.

Celery: Look for celery that has thick and solid stalks and crisp leaves. Refrigerate.

Chili peppers: Look for chili peppers that are smooth and deep colored, with no soft spots. Refrigerate.

Collard greens: Look for collard greens that are crisp and green, not limp or yellowed. Refrigerate.

Corn: Look for corn that has fresh green husks, undamaged golden brown silk fibers, and plump unblemished kernels. Refrigerate.

Cucumbers: Look for cucumbers that are firm, smooth, and shiny, with no soft spots. Refrigerate.

Eggplant: Look for an eggplant that is heavy and shiny, with tight smooth skin and a bright green stem cap. Refrigerate.

Garlic: Look for garlic that is firm and dry, with a papery sheath free of green sprouts. Store in a cool, dry place in an open jar or net bag.

Green onions: Look for green onions with crisp, bright green tops and firm white bases. Refrigerate.

Kale: Look for kale that has tender green leaves, without yellowing or drying. Refrigerate.

Lettuce: Look for lettuce that is crisp and firm, with no brown spots or streaks. Refrigerate, uncut and unwashed.

Mushrooms: Look for mushrooms that are firm, with closed caps and no soft spots. Refrigerate.

Okra: Look for okra with firm, brightly colored pods that are 2 to 3 inches long. Refrigerate.

Onions: Look for onions that are firm, with dry papery skins, free of sprouting and spots. Store in a cool, dry place in an open jar or net bag.

Parsley: Look for parsley that is bright green and free of yellowing. Refrigerate.

Parsnips: Look for parsnips that are firm, smooth, well shaped, and small to medium in size. Refrigerate.

Potatoes: Look for potatoes that are firm, smooth, well shaped, and free of soft dark areas, cracks, green patches, and sprouts. Store in a cool, dark place with good air flow, not in the refrigerator.

Pumpkin: Look for a pumpkin that is heavy for its size, with clear, unbroken skin and no soft spots. Store in a cool place or at room temperature.

Radishes: Look for radishes that are firm, smooth, and well formed, with crisp green leaves, if attached. Remove and discard leaves. Refrigerate.

Rutabaga: Look for rutabagas that are smooth, firm, and heavy for their size. Refrigerate.

Spinach: Look for spinach that is crisp and deep green, without yellow spots. Refrigerate.

Squash: Look for summer squash (such as yellow crook-neck, pattypan, straightneck, and zucchini) that is small, with bright-colored, taut skin free of spots and bruises. Refrigerate. Look for winter squash (such as acorn, butter-nut, hubbard, and spaghetti) that is heavy for its size, with a hard, deep-colored rind free of gashes, mold, or soft spots. Store in a cool, dark place with good air flow.

Sweet potatoes: Look for sweet potatoes that are firm, with smooth, unbruised skins. Store in a cool, dark place with good air flow.

Tomatillos: Look for tomatillos that are firm, with dry, tight-fitting husks. Refrigerate.

Tomatoes: Look for tomatoes that are firm, plump, well formed, smooth, and free of soft spots or bruises. Ripen at room temperature. Tomatoes lose flavor when refrigerated.

Turnip greens: Look for turnip greens that are crisp, green, and free of yellowing. Refrigerate.

Turnips: Look for turnips that are firm, smooth, small, and heavy for their size. Refrigerate.

Water chestnuts: Look for water chestnuts that are firm, with no sign of shriveling. Refrigerate.

Watercress: Look for watercress that is crisp and deep green, without yellowing. Refrigerate.

Yams: Look for yams with tight, smooth, unbruised skins. Store in a cool, dark place with good air flow. Do not refrigerate.

Using Vegetables

■ Add vegetables to an omelet or scrambled eggs. Try onions, peppers, mushrooms, and/or tomatoes.

■ Replace some of the meat in tomato sauce with onions, peppers, mushrooms, eggplant, and/or zucchini.

■ Put extra vegetables on a pizza.

■ Add vegetables to sandwiches. Try alfalfa sprouts, sliced red onion, sliced cucumbers, sliced zucchini, raw spinach leaves, and/or red peppers.

■ Serve more raw and slightly cooked vegetables.

■ Leave skins on potatoes, tomatoes, cucumbers, and other vegetables.

Cooking with Less Salt

Salt occurs naturally in foods, usually in small amounts. Most of the salt in our diet comes from the salt added to processed and prepared foods. Most Americans eat too much salt. Foods high in salt include canned foods, cured and smoked meats (bacon, sausage, salami, hot dogs, and bologna), pickles, salad dressings, mustard, breakfast cereals, cheese, frozen dinners, and salty snacks.

Here are some tips for choosing frozen dinners, canned foods, and snack foods, and for cutting salt when preparing foods.

Choosing Frozen Dinners
Select frozen dinners that have

■ Less than 800 milligrams of sodium per serving.

■ Less than 400 calories per serving.

■ No more than 10 grams of fat per serving.

■ Less than 50 milligrams of cholesterol per serving.

Choosing Canned Foods
Choose unsalted canned vegetables and beans. Rinse salted canned foods (vegetables, beans, fish, shellfish, and meats) with cold water for 1 minute to remove some of the sodium. Choose unsalted canned tomato sauce, paste, and puree and unsalted broth. Choose canned soups with less than 400 milligrams of sodium and no more than 3 grams of fat per serving.

Choosing Snack Foods
Look for crackers, chips, popcorn, and pretzels that are unsalted or low in salt and that have 1 to 2 grams of fat per serving.

Cutting Salt When Preparing Foods
■ Use low-sodium or reduced-sodium soy sauce, steak sauce, catsup, and barbecue sauce.

■ Dilute regular soy sauce with an equal amount of water or wine.

■ Cook with unsalted butter or margarine, or use vegetable oil, which is salt-free.

■ Substitute chicken or turkey for prosciutto, ham, or other salty, cured meats.

■ Cook with reduced-sodium cheese, salad dressing, and mayonnaise.

■ Use lemon juice, flavored vinegars, pepper, garlic, and other herbs and spices in place of salt.

- Use garlic, onion, and celery powders in place of garlic, onion, and celery salts.

- Skip the salt when preparing pasta, rice, vegetables, and hot cereal.

- Omit salt in recipes. In some recipes, you can use half the amount of salt called for. In other recipes, you can leave the salt out altogether. Be careful, though—many baking recipes, such as those made with yeast, need salt for the recipe to work.

Cooking with Herbs and Spices

Herbs and spices can flavor your food in place of salt, fat, or sugar. The recipes in this book use many different herbs and spices to flavor food.

One way to make herbs and spices release their flavor is to heat them. You can do this by sauteing them; boiling them in soups, stews, or sauces; or putting them on meats or vegetables before cooking. When adding herbs and spices to soups or stews, do so during the last hour of cooking to preserve their flavor.

Another way to release the flavor of herbs and spices is to crush them before you use them. You can crush herbs and spices with a mortar and pestle, blender, or chopper.

Soaking herbs and spices in a cold liquid also releases their flavor. But this takes much longer—days to weeks. This method can be used to make flavored oils and vinegars, salad dressings, and marinades.

If a recipe calls for fresh herbs and you will be using dried herbs, use 1/3 the amount called for. If a recipe calls for dried herbs and you will be using fresh herbs, use three times the amount called for. If you are trying an herb or spice for the first time, start by adding 1/4 teaspoon of dried herbs or 1 teaspoon of chopped fresh herbs for every four servings of food.

Buy fresh herbs no more than a few days before you plan to use them. Keep them wrapped in a damp paper towel in a plastic bag. Buy dried herbs and spices in small amounts, because they lose flavor the longer they sit around.

Cooking with Sugars and Sugar Substitutes

Sugars

The latest American Diabetes Association nutritional guidelines allow sugars (table sugar, brown sugar, honey, and molasses, for example) as part of the total carbohydrate in a diabetes meal plan. Although sugars add sweetness and texture to foods, especially baked goods, they also add empty calories.

You can reduce the sugars called for in many baking recipes by 1/4 to 1/2 without affecting the quality. A general guideline is to use 1/4 cup or less of added sugars for each cup of flour.

Fresh fruit is a natural replacement for all or part of the sugar in a recipe. Try applesauce in baked goods, fresh fruit instead of syrup on pancakes, and fruit juice in salad dressings. Be aware that fruit juice or fruit juice concentrates have more nutrients than sugar, such as vitamin C, but they provide the same amount of calories and carbohydrate, and they raise blood glucose about as high as sugar does.

Fructose is the sugar found in fruits and honey. It is also extracted as a sweetener. Fructose may cause a smaller rise in your blood glucose level than other sugars. But large amounts of fructose may increase your cholesterol levels. Because of these findings, the American Diabetes Association cautions that there is no reason to use fructose in place of other sugars.

Some herbs and spices can be used in place of sugar in recipes. You've probably heard of or used herbs and spices like cinnamon, nutmeg, ginger, cloves, coriander seeds, and mint. But have you tried lemon-flavored herbs like lemon balm, lemon basil, lemon thyme, and lemon verbena? Try pineapple sage for a pineapple taste, or try fennel seeds or anise seeds for a licorice taste.

Sugar Substitutes
The American Diabetes Association approves the use of three sugar substitutes in moderate amounts. These are aspartame (Nutrasweet, Equal), saccharin (Sweet'N Low), and acesulfame potassium (Sweet One). Sugar substitutes have very few calories and will not affect your blood glucose level. Sugar substitutes are useful for making foods taste sweet without added carbohydrates or calories.

Acesulfame potassium can be used in baking and cooking. However, the texture of baked goods made with acesulfame potassium will not be the same as those made with sugar. You might try using half sugar and half acesulfame potassium.

Aspartame can be added to cold foods or to hot foods after they have been cooked. Usually, it should not be used during baking or cooking. Aspartame tends to lose its sweetness when heated or is present for a long time in a cold or hot liquid.

Saccharin, too, may lose its sweetness at high temperatures or during long cooking times, such as baking. It is best to add saccharin to hot foods toward the end of cooking or right afterward.

Buying Desserts

One advantage to making your own cakes, cookies, pies, and other desserts is that you can control how much sugar and fat go into them. When you buy prepared baked goods, you need to watch out for not only sugar, but also fat.

Look for baked goods with 3 grams or less of fat per 100 calories. And if you like your pie à la mode, look for frozen desserts (yogurt, ice cream, or sherbet) with 3 grams or less of fat and 100 to 150 calories per 1/2-cup serving. Avoid frozen desserts that contain cream of coconut, coconut milk, or coconut oil.

Great Cooking Techniques

Dinner in a Bag

Just about everything you can boil or bake tastes wonderful when you prepare it inside parchment. Parchment-wrapped foods retain their vitamins and other nutrients better than boiled foods. Foods become more flavorful as they absorb spices and herbs. Perhaps best of all, parchment doesn't need to be coated with oil or fat, and properly cooked food doesn't stick to it.

Parchment is reusable, too. Just rinse it off and let it dry. Parchment also makes great lining material for casseroles, cake pans, and cookie sheets. It can even serve as a cover, tucked over a roast or casserole. You can buy a roll of parchment in a cutter-edge box or in precut squares, oblongs, or circles. It's readily available in many cooking specialty stores.

If you are pressed for time, prepare your parchment packets, partially cook them, then refrigerate them until you are ready to finish the cooking. Or freeze the packets, uncooked but well wrapped, then let them thaw in the refrigerator before you use them. Bring a parchment-wrapped packet to school or work, refrigerate, then simply set it in the microwave to cook or reheat for lunch. Cut parchment into shapes and use them as stencils on top of cakes, or make food decorations out of them. You can even make flowers out of parchment and set them on the plate before you serve your guests.

There are several ways to wrap the parchment packets. For a poaching bag, place the food in the center of the paper. Bring the corners together, twist, and tie. To make a heart packet, fold the parchment in half and cut a lopsided "C."

Place the food near the fold. Make 1/4-inch folds that overlap to seal the edges. A circle can also be folded in half and sealed the same way for a more circular packet. For a lunch wrap, place the food in the center of the paper. Bring the long sides together at the top and make a 1/2-inch fold. Continue folding down until the fold is flat against the food. At each end, make 1/2-inch folds and continue folding until the ends are against the food. Secure the ends with paper clips.

Be generous when you cut your pieces of parchment. It's good to make each sheet a bit more than twice the size of the food that will go into it. Fold the sheet in half and crease it well so you have a clear center fold line; that will help you place the food properly. Then crease the folds well as you prepare the packet for cooking.

Poaching Bag

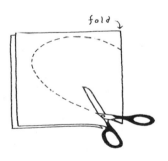

Try some of the following recipes to get you started cooking with parchment!

Heart Packet

Lunch Wrap

Chicken en Papillote

Cooking parchment
2 lemons, peeled and thinly sliced
4 cloves garlic, thinly sliced
1/2 tsp fennel seeds
4 sprigs fresh thyme
2 tsp olive oil
2 boneless, skinless chicken breasts, halved
Fresh ground pepper to taste
1/2 cup white vermouth, other dry white wine, or white grape juice
4 sprigs parsley

1. Preheat the oven to 400°F. Tear off 4 sheets of parchment, each about 10 inches long, or double the size of the food that will go onto each sheet.

2. Divide the lemon, garlic, fennel, and thyme evenly on each piece of parchment. Drizzle the olive oil equally over each. Place a piece of chicken on each sheet and season with pepper. Pour 2 Tbsp wine over each piece of chicken, and set a sprig of parsley on top.

4 servings
Serving size: 1/2 chicken breast
Lean Meat Exchange.......3
Calories 179
Total Fat.........................5 g
  Saturated Fat............1 g
  Calories from Fat......48
Cholesterol ....72 mg
Sodium.......................71 mg
Carbohydrate.................2 g
  Dietary Fiber..............0 g
  Sugars.....................1 g
Protein.........................27 g

3. Fold the parchment packets with well-creased folds according to the style you choose. Place the packets on a baking sheet. Bake for 20–25 minutes. To serve, transfer each packet to an individual plate.

Fish en Papillote

Cooking parchment
4 rainbow trout or small sea bass (about 6 oz each after they
    are cleaned and boned)
4 slices whole-wheat bread
2 tsp olive oil
2 tsp chopped fresh dill
1 small onion, diced
1 tsp lemon juice (optional)
Fresh ground pepper to taste

1. Preheat the oven to 350°F. Tear off 4 sheets of parchment, each a little more than double the size of one deboned fish. Rinse each fish inside and out with cool water; pat dry.

2. Process the bread in a blender or food processor until you have soft bread crumbs. Combine the bread crumbs with the remaining ingredients. Stuff the cavity of each fish with the bread mixture.

4 servings
Serving size: 1 fish
Starch Exchange................1
Lean Meat Exchange.......4
Fat Exchange..................1/2
Calories 334
Total Fat.......................14 g
    Saturated Fat...........2 g
    Calories from Fat.....126
Cholesterol...............92 mg
Sodium ....234 mg
Carbohydrate...............15 g
    Dietary Fiber.............2 g
    Sugars ....2 g
Protein...........................36 g

3. Wrap each fish in a piece of parchment (a semicircle fold works well). Bake the wrapped fish for about 15–20 minutes, turning once or twice. The fish will be mildly flavored and moist when done. To serve, transfer each packet to an individual plate.

Posh Squash

Cooking parchment
1 Tbsp brown sugar
1 Tbsp low-calorie margarine, melted
2 acorn squash, peeled and cut into 1/2-inch chunks

1. Preheat the oven to 350°F. Tear off 5 sheets of parchment, each about 10 inches long, or double the size of the food that will go onto each sheet.

2. Mix the brown sugar and margarine. Drizzle the mixture onto the squash chunks and toss to mix. Divide the squash mixture equally among the 5 pieces of parchment. Fold as you choose, using well-creased folds.

5 servings
Serving size: 1/5 recipe
Starch Exchange..............1
Calories....................88
Total Fat...................2 g
  Saturated Fat...........0 g
  Calories from Fat........21
Cholesterol.............0 mg
Sodium.................33 mg
Carbohydrate.............18 g
  Dietary Fiber............5 g
  Sugars...................8 g
Protein....................1 g

3. Bake the squash for 50–60 minutes. To serve, transfer each packet to an individual plate.

Fruit Fold

Cooking parchment
4 orange slices, with rind (washed)
1 lemon slice, with rind (washed)
1/2 cup pineapple chunks (if using canned, rinse well)
1 large apple, peeled and cubed
1/4 tsp cinnamon, or to taste
1/2 tsp sugar
1 Tbsp shredded coconut (optional)

1. Preheat the oven to 325°F. Tear off 4 sheets of parchment, each about 8 inches long, or double the size of the food that will go onto each sheet.

2. Divide the fruit evenly on the parchment sheets. Add the cinnamon and sugar (and coconut, if desired). Fold up the sides of the parchment as you choose, using well-creased folds.

4 servings
Serving size: 1/4 recipe
Fruit Exchange 1 1/2
Calories 78
Total Fat.........................0 g
   Saturated Fat...........0 g
   Calories from Fat 5
Cholesterol ....0 mg
Sodium ....1 mg
Carbohydrate ....21 g
   Dietary Fiber ....3 g
   Sugars ....17 g
Protein ....1 g

3. Place the packages on a baking sheet and bake 8–10 minutes. To serve, transfer each packet to a plate. (Open carefully; the fruit gives off liquid as it bakes.)

Apple Wrap

Cooking parchment
4 large, Red Delicious apples, washed and unpeeled
1 Tbsp sugar
1 tsp cinnamon
1 Tbsp unsalted butter, melted
1 Tbsp walnut meal (or finely cut walnuts)

1. Preheat the oven to 375°F. Tear off 4 pieces of parchment, each about 15 inches long, or double the size of the apple that will go on it.

2. Cut the top off each apple and set the tops aside. Remove the core of each apple, leaving sides and bottom intact. Set each apple on its own piece of parchment.

3. Mix sugar, cinnamon, butter and walnut meal together. Dribble an equal amount of the mixture inside each apple. Wrap each apple in a "chocolate kiss" packet, twisting the top well. Bake for 45 minutes.

4 servings
Serving size: 1 apple
Fruit Exchange..................2
Fat Exchange 1
Calories 174
Total Fat.......................5 g
   Saturated Fat...........1 g
   Calories from Fat 44
Cholesterol ....8 mg
Sodium........................0 mg
Carbohydrate..............35 g
   Dietary Fiber.............6 g
   Sugars....................29 g
Protein ....1 g

Add Verve with Herbs

There is nothing like fresh-cut herbs to add interesting new flavors to your meals. Be adventurous—try different herbs with different foods. Some herbs are pungent, so you may want to try small amounts at first, then gradually increase the quantities to a level you like. If a recipe calls for a dried herb, use three times the amount of the fresh herb. Because of their different textures and colors, herbs also make attractive garnishes.

You might enjoy growing your own herbs. To prepare herbs for storage, harvest plants growing in the garden just after the dew dries in the morning, but before it gets hot. Cut the stems long and tie them together. Place the bouquet of herbs upside down in a paper bag and hang it to dry where there is good air circulation. Leave it for several days. When the bouquet is completely dry, remove the leaves from the stems. Store the dried leaves in plastic bags or in a jar with a tight lid. Sage, basil, oregano, thyme, and marjoram dry well.

Try some of the following herbs in your favorite recipes:

- **Chives,** a perennial, form a neat 8- to 10-inch-high border, but can also be grown in a small pot because they don't spread rapidly. The slender leaves will stay green all winter in mild climates, and the plant will produce lovely lavender flower heads. Their long green stems resemble very small green onion tops. Chopped, they add spirit to mashed potatoes or omelets.
- **Dill** is popular in salads and as a garnish for fish or poultry dishes. The delicate leaves should be harvested when the plants are young and tender. You can harvest the seed heads when they are in bloom and use the seeds to season vinegar for marinated cucumber salad.

- **Marjoram** is a small, compact plant that's easy to grow and goes well with meats, vegetables, and soups. It tastes best when its leaves are harvested before the plant blooms.
- **Mint** comes in a seemingly endless variety of flavors: peppermint, spearmint, apple, orange, and even chocolate. Mint leaves make an excellent garnish for iced beverages, fruit, and puddings. Mint grows well in moist, somewhat shady locations.
- **Rosemary** is a small, tender, evergreen shrub. In fact, it is sometimes sold in pots during the holiday season to be used as miniature Christmas trees. It's good in chicken, fish, and pasta dishes.
- **Sage** comes in several varieties and will usually survive mild winters outdoors. It goes well with poultry or pork and adds a festive look to a dish. The most common variety of sage has grayish green leaves, but some sage varieties have attractive variegated white/green or green/purple leaves. Pineapple sage has bright green leaves and a nice pineapple fragrance. It also produces small scarlet flower spikes. However, pineapple sage tends to be intolerant of temperature extremes.
- **Sweet basil** is a favorite annual that comes in several varieties, with heights that vary from 1 to 2 feet. You might also want to try lemon basil, with its small, delicate, light green leaves. Basil is most flavorful if harvested before the plant blooms, but it's quite pretty when in bloom. Basil is a versatile herb and can be used to season meat, poultry, fish, vegetables, or soups. As with most herbs, you harvest the leaves.
- **Thyme** and **oregano** are low-spreading, perennial herbs. Thyme needs well-drained soil and makes a pretty border or ground cover. The flavor of thyme and oregano varies somewhat, depending on the variety, but all varieties enhance the taste of soups, stews, and many vegetables. Fresh oregano is great for pasta dishes.

Roast Pork Tenderloin with Rosemary

2 sprigs fresh rosemary
1 1/2 lb pork tenderloin

1. Preheat the oven to 325°F. Place the rosemary sprigs between the two parts of the tenderloin. Wrap the tenderloin in aluminum foil and place in a small baking pan. Roast for about 1 hour, or until the internal temperature of meat is 165°F.

2. Carefully remove the foil and allow the meat to roast uncovered for an additional 10 minutes, or until browned. Remove from the oven and allow to cool slightly. Remove the rosemary sprigs, slice, and serve.

8 servings
Serving size: 2 oz
Lean Meat Exchange 2
Calories 107
Total Fat.......................3 g
    Calories from Fat.......27
Cholesterol ....60 mg
Sodium.......................40 mg
Carbohydrate ....0 g
    Dietary Fiber..............0 g
Protein ....11 g

Individual Savory Turkey Loaves

1 lb fresh ground turkey (or 93% lean packaged)
1/4 cup soft whole-wheat bread crumbs
1/4 cup egg substitute
1/3 cup finely chopped onion
1 Tbsp chopped fresh oregano
1 Tbsp chopped fresh basil
1 tsp chopped fresh thyme
Nonstick cooking spray

1. Preheat the oven to 325°F. Combine all ingredients except the nonstick cooking spray and mix thoroughly. Divide the mixture into 6 servings and shape each into a small loaf. Each loaf will be about the size of a muffin.

2. Spray an 8-inch-square baking pan with nonstick cooking spray. Place the loaves in the pan. Bake, uncovered, for 50–55 minutes.

6 servings
Serving size: 1 loaf
Lean Meat Exchange 2
Calories.........................133
Total Fat ....7 g
    Calories from Fat......63
Cholesterol ....56 mg
Sodium......................99 mg
Carbohydrate.................2 g
    Dietary Fiber.............0 g
Protein............................15 g

Orange Mint Slaw

1/2 cup orange juice
1 Tbsp vinegar
1 Tbsp fresh mint leaves
2 tsp sugar substitute
3 cups raw cabbage, shredded
4 Tbsp raisins
1 cup fresh orange sections, chopped

1. Place the orange juice, vinegar, mint leaves, and sugar substitute in a blender or food processor. Process the dressing for a few seconds, until the mint leaves are finely chopped.

2. Place the shredded cabbage in a large bowl. Pour the salad dressing over the cabbage and toss well to coat. Garnish with raisins and orange sections.

4 servings
Serving size: 1/4 recipe
Fruit Exchange....................1
Vegetable Exchange...........1
Calories.............................80
Total Fat.........................0 g
    Calories from Fat.........0
Cholesterol..................0 mg
Sodium..........................11 mg
Carbohydrate...............20 g
    Dietary Fiber..............3 g
Protein............................2 g

Herb Spread

16 Tbsp fat-free cream cheese
2 tsp chopped fresh dill
1 Tbsp chopped fresh chives
1 Tbsp chopped parsley
1 Tbsp chopped shallots

Allow the cream cheese to soften at room temperature. Mix in the herbs and put the mixture in a container with a lid. Refrigerate for 24 hours before serving.

16 servings
Serving size: 1 Tbsp
Free Food
Calories................................14
Total Fat..........................0 g
   Calories from Fat.........0
Cholesterol ....3 mg
Sodium.......................85 mg
Carbohydrate ....0 g
   Dietary Fiber..............0 g
Protein ....2 g

The World's Greatest Pasta

Making Basic Pasta

To make pasta, you can use virtually any combination of flours that equals 2 cups. The best choice may be durum wheat flour. The best of the durum is called semolina. Start with no more than half durum semolina flour in your dough—it's very coarse and difficult to knead.

Here are a few likely flour combinations: 1 cup durum semolina flour and 1 cup white or whole-wheat flour, 1/2 cup semolina flour and 1 1/2 cups white flour, 1 cup whole-wheat flour and 1 cup white flour, 2 cups white flour, or 2 cups cake flour.

Use any combination of liquid to equal 1/2 to 3/4 cups of liquid. This may include eggs, egg substitute, or even baby food. The exact amount of liquid will vary with the type of flour used and the humidity of the kitchen.

You may also use any number of optional ingredients in the dough, such as 1/4 tsp salt; 1/4 tsp black or cayenne pepper; 1/4 tsp saffron threads dissolved in 1 tsp hot water; or 2 tsp finely chopped herbs, such as parsley, marjoram, basil, sage, rosemary, thyme, tarragon, or fennel. These ingredients do not alter the nutritional content or the exchange values of the pasta.

Mixing the Dough
By Hand
1. On a clean dry surface or in a large bowl, mound the flour and make a deep well in the center. Put the liquid (including eggs) into the well and beat the liquids lightly inside the well.

2. Add any other ingredients to the well, and—using a circular motion—draw the flour into the center of the well from around the sides. Continue mixing in this fashion until the dough is too stiff for you to go on. Lightly dust a clean, dry table or board with flour.

3. Pat the dough into a ball and knead it, adding flour to the dough as it becomes sticky. To knead, dig the palm of your hand into the dough and push outward. Keep turning the dough around so you are kneading different sides, and continue kneading until the dough is smooth, elastic, and no longer sticky, about 10 minutes.

4. Continue lightly dusting the table with flour if the dough sticks to it. If the ball of dough is crumbly, add a few drops of water and knead it to mix the water and flour together well. You are now ready to roll out the dough.

Using a Food Processor
1. Combine the flour and egg in the food processor and process until the mixture looks like cornmeal, about 5 to 7 seconds.

2. With the motor running, add the liquid and any other ingredients. Run the processor briefly, until the dough forms a ball that is well blended but not sticky. If the ball is sticky, add flour. If it is crumbly, add another drop or two of liquid.

3. Turn the dough out onto a dry, floured surface and knead it a few times until it is smooth.

Using a Bread-Baking Machine
1. Set the machine on dough cycle and put all ingredients into the machine.

2. Once the machine has begun mixing and blending, peek in. If the dough looks very dry, add 1/2 tsp water. If it looks very wet, add flour, beginning with 1 Tbsp. You want the dough to collect in a shiny ball that resembles bread dough.

3. This method takes about 1 hour, but makes an excellent dough and leaves the kitchen clean.

Rolling the Dough

1. Divide the prepared dough into fourths. Keep the unrolled portions covered so they won't dry out. If you plan to use a manual or electric pasta machine, you can roll the dough out immediately. However, if you are using a rolling pin, let the dough rest for 20 minutes first.

2. On a floured surface, roll out 1/4 of the dough into a 5 x 7-inch rectangle, about 1/16th inch thick. The dough will be elastic enough not to tear. If the dough becomes sticky at any point, add a little flour. (It's extremely difficult to cut strips from soft, sticky dough.)

3. Allow the rolled-out dough to rest, uncovered, while you roll out the rest of the dough. Let each portion dry until it begins to feel leathery, about 5 to 10 minutes.

Cutting the Pasta into Strips

1. Sprinkle a clean, dry surface with a light coating of flour. Start to roll up the dough at the narrow end of the rectangle, and roll it as you would a jelly roll. The dough should not be easy to roll, but rather elastic and a little resistant.

2. Once you have the dough rolled up, take a serrated knife and cut it crosswise into strips (that is, noodles). Cut the strips as wide or narrow as you wish. You can shape the

pasta any way you want. For example, wrap the strips around a chopstick and slide them off to make curlicues. It takes practice, but it's fun!

3. To get the best taste from your homemade pasta, cook and serve it immediately. Or let the newly made pasta dry for an hour. Then place it in a plastic bag and store it in the refrigerator for 2 days, or freeze it for up to 2 months. When you are ready to use frozen pasta, do not thaw it before plunging it into boiling water.

Cooking Homemade Pasta

1. There are two secrets to cooking perfect pasta, whether it's homemade or store-bought: plenty of water and careful timing. Use at least 4 qt water for every 1/2 lb dry pasta. Make sure the saucepan is large enough to allow the pasta to float free while cooking.

2. If you are adding salt to the cooking water, don't add it until the water comes to a rolling boil. When the water does come to a boil, add the pasta all at once, then stir vigorously, reaching down to the bottom of the pan with the spoon to keep the pasta from sticking.

3. Allow the water to return to a rolling boil. Begin the timing once the water begins to boil again. Commercial pasta takes 7–8 minutes to cook; fresh pasta usually takes no more than 1–3 minutes. However, if you have allowed the pasta to dry or have frozen it, allow 3 to 5 minutes for cooking, but no longer. Don't rinse the pasta after draining it unless you are using it in a cold dish.

Basic Egg Pasta

1 cup durum semolina flour
1 cup enriched flour
1/2 tsp salt
1/2–3/4 cups water
2 eggs

Follow the basic instructions on p. 39.

12 servings
Serving size: 1/2 cup
Starch Exchange.................1
Calories............................88
Total Fat ....1 g
   Saturated Fat...........0 g
   Calories from Fat.........9
Cholesterol...............35 mg
Sodium ....100 mg
Carbohydrate...............16 g
   Dietary Fiber ....1 g
   Sugars.........................0 g
Protein ....3 g

Spinach or Carrot Pasta

1/2 cup durum semolina flour
1 1/2 cups enriched white flour
3–6 Tbsp water
1/2 cup egg substitute
2 Tbsp pureed spinach or carrot baby food
1/2 tsp salt

Follow the basic instructions on p. 39.

12 servings
Serving size: 1/2 cup
Starch Exchange.................1
Calories 81
Total Fat..........................0 g
   Saturated Fat...........0 g
   Calories from Fat.........0
Cholesterol ....0 mg
Sodium ....104 mg
Carbohydrate................16 g
   Dietary Fiber ....1 g
   Sugars...........................1 g
Protein ....3 g

Fresh Tomato Sauce

2 Tbsp olive oil
1/2 cup chopped onion
1 carrot, finely chopped
2 celery stalks, finely chopped
1/2 green pepper, finely chopped
8 medium fresh tomatoes, peeled, cored, and chopped (or 1
    29-oz can whole tomatoes, chopped, reserve liquid)
1/4 cup tomato paste
1 cup water (omit if using canned tomatoes)
1 tsp ground basil or 4 fresh basil leaves, washed
1/4 tsp oregano
1/8 tsp pepper

1. Heat the oil in a large non-stick skillet and saute the onion, carrot, celery, and green pepper until the onion is translucent, about 3–5 minutes. Add the remaining ingredients except the pepper, and stir the mixture until well blended.

2. When the sauce begins to simmer gently, cover and let simmer for 30–40 minutes, stirring occasionally. Season with pepper and serve.

8 servings
Serving size: 1/2 cup
Vegetable Exchange..........2
Fat Exchange..................1/2
Calories.............................71
Total Fat........................4 g
    Saturated Fat............1 g
    Calories from Fat......38
Cholesterol.................0 mg
Sodium....................245 mg
Carbohydrate................9 g
    Dietary Fiber............2 g
    Sugars.....................5 g
Protein..........................2 g

Food-Mix Magic

Did you ever wish you could walk into your kitchen, wave a magic wand, and create a healthy, nourishing meal for your family? Well, you can, by making your own premade food mixes. These aren't frozen dinners or cans of soup or stew—these are dry mixes, the kind you use to make cakes or biscuits, or to coat chicken and fish before baking.

Making your own mixes also eliminates the old trade-off between convenience and nutrition. While commercial mixes can save you lots of time, many of these mixes, unfortunately, are high in sodium and fat. Your own mixes provide convenience along with the peace of mind that comes along with serving healthy foods. There's still another bonus: homemade mixes offer you a chance to be creative, choose your own seasonings, experiment with spices, and discover new tastes to zip up your old standbys.

The following recipes offer a variety of basic mixes, each with the same simple instructions: mix all ingredients well. Store in a plastic bag closed with a twist tie or in a tightly sealed jar. Keep refrigerated. Your mixes will be tastiest if used within 2 to 3 months.

Jamaican Coating Mix
1 1/2 cups All-Around Coating Mix
1 Tbsp instant minced onion
2 tsp thyme
1 tsp sugar
1/2 tsp pepper
1 tsp allspice
1/2 tsp cinnamon
1/2 tsp nutmeg
1/2 tsp cayenne pepper

All-Around Coating Mix
1 1/2 cups bread crumbs (different breads will add their own textures and tastes)
1/4 tsp pepper
1/2 tsp salt

Mexican Coating Mix
1 1/2 cups All-Around Coating Mix
1/2 tsp garlic powder
1/2 tsp onion powder
1/2 tsp cumin
1/2 tsp coriander

Chicken Coating Mix
1 1/2 cups All-Around Coating Mix
1/2 tsp poultry seasoning
1/2 tsp thyme
1/8 tsp cayenne pepper

Mediterranean Coating Mix
1 1/2 cups All-Around Coating Mix
1 tsp oregano
1 tsp basil
1/2 tsp thyme
1/8 tsp cayenne pepper

Great Basic General Mix
2 cups flour
3 tsp baking powder
1/2 tsp baking soda
1/2 tsp salt

Stir 'n' Drop Biscuits

2 1/4 cups Great Basic General Mix
1 cup skim milk
1/4 cup vegetable oil
Nonstick cooking spray

1. Preheat the oven to 450°F. Measure the Great Basic General Mix into a bowl.

2. In a separate bowl, combine the milk and oil. Pour into the Great Basic General Mix. Stir with a fork until the mixture pulls away from the sides of the bowl.

3. Spray a cookie sheet lightly with nonstick cooking spray. Drop the mix in 12 equal portions onto the cookie sheet. Bake 8–10 minutes.

12 servings
Serving size: 1 biscuit
Starch Exchange..............1
Fat Exchange 1
Calories...........................132
Total Fat ....5 g
   Calories from Fat 45
Cholesterol ....0 mg
Sodium ....248 mg
Carbohydrate...............19 g
   Dietary Fiber..............0 g
Protein ....3 g

Broccoli Cheese Pie

Nonstick cooking spray
1/3 cup chopped onion
1 cup shredded Swiss cheese
1 10-oz pkg frozen chopped broccoli, thawed and drained
3 eggs
1 1/2 cups skim milk
3/4 cup Great Basic General Mix
1/4 tsp salt
1/4 tsp pepper
1/8 tsp cayenne pepper

1. Preheat the oven to 400°F. Spray a 10-inch pie pan with nonstick cooking spray. Combine the onion, cheese, and broccoli; place the mixture in the pie pan.

2. In a medium bowl, beat the eggs with the milk. Add the Great Basic General Mix, salt, pepper, and cayenne pepper. Stir until the mixture is smooth. Pour over the broccoli.

3. Bake for 35 minutes, or until a knife inserted in the middle comes out clean. Allow to stand 5 minutes before cutting.

8 servings
Serving size: 1 slice
Starch Exchange..............1
Medium-Fat Meat
     Exchange 1
Calories..........................140
Total Fat..........................5 g
     Calories from Fat 45
Cholesterol................111 mg
Sodium....................340 mg
Carbohydrate...............14 g
     Dietary Fiber.............0 g
Protein..........................9 g

Banana Bread

Nonstick cooking spray
3 medium bananas, well ripened
2 eggs
1/2 cup buttermilk
2 1/2 cups Great Basic General Mix
1/2 cup sugar

1. Preheat the oven to 350°F. Spray a 9 x 5 x 3-inch loaf pan with nonstick cooking spray.

2. In a large mixing bowl, cream the bananas to a smooth paste with the back of a spoon. Add the eggs, beating to combine with the banana paste. Stir in the buttermilk. Add the Great Basic General Mix and sugar and mix well.

12 servings
Serving size: 1 slice
Starch Exchange 2
Calories...........................185
Total Fat ....2 g
   Calories from Fat 18
Cholesterol ....36 mg
Sodium.....................155 mg
Carbohydrate ....38 g
   Dietary Fiber ....2 g
Protein ....5 g

3. Pour the batter into the loaf pan. Bake for 50–55 minutes or until a toothpick inserted into the center comes out clean. Cool for 5 minutes, remove from pan, and cool until ready to serve.

The Pressure Is On!

If you haven't used a pressure cooker lately—or ever—you are in for a pleasant surprise. This tool can help you create healthy, tasty, and low-cost meals for one person or for the whole family.

Pressure-cooked foods can be so low in fat that they fit into just about any meal plan. And even traditionally slow-cooking choices such as red meat, chicken, dried beans, or brown rice are ready for the table in about one-third the usual time. Steam cooking also softens vegetable and meat fibers, automatically tenderizing inexpensive cuts of meat.

Pressure cookers work by building up steam inside the cooker. That internal steam cooks the food. Some cooks, though they may not admit it, are afraid of a pressure cooker. Once you understand the built-in precautions, however, you can see that it is a safe addition to your kitchen.

The cooker has a tightly closed lid sealed with a rubber ring. No steam will build up if the lid is not properly closed and locked into position. The cooker also has a vent that releases steam if the pressure inside climbs too high. On the lid is a pressure regulator that shows the internal pressure. While some specialized cookers have a gauge to tell you the pressure, most regulators rock and "chug" along as the cooker cooks, letting you know all is well.

While there are no tricks to using a pressure cooker, it is important to take a few minutes to read the instruction book that accompanies it. You'll learn some basics, such as how to lock the lid in place, how to gauge the pressure inside the cooker, and how to choose an appropriate method for allowing the pressure to subside.

Pressure Cookers

You'll also become familiar with the proper amount of liquid to add. Generally, cookers don't use much liquid, and overdoing it is a mistake. The plus side is that this kind of cooking retains the vitamins and minerals that are often poured down the drain. And, because the cooker takes virtually any kind of liquid from water to soup, you can get a lot of flavor versatility.

There are many pressure cooker models on the market with various features to choose from. However, all are safe and work well when used as directed, so choose the one that suits you best. Do make sure you get a heat-proof handle, however. Pressure cookers come with a removable rack. These racks are useful for setting food above the liquid, if that is what the recipe calls for.

It's a good idea to buy a large cooker, with a capacity of at least 6 quarts. This allows you to use your pressure cooker for a wide selection of dishes. Keep in mind that instructions will tell you not to fill the cooker to the top—not even more than halfway—so a large cooker might not make as much as you think.

Try some of the following recipes in your new pressure cooker!

Seafood Gumbo

2 tsp olive oil
2 medium onions, chopped
1 cup canned tomatoes
1 clove garlic
1 Tbsp chopped parsley
1 tsp thyme
2 cups low-fat, low-sodium chicken broth
1 lb orange roughy or other firm, boneless fish
1 cup chopped celery
2 cups frozen okra
1/2 large green pepper, chopped
1/4 cup tomato paste
12 oz frozen, cooked shrimp

1. Preheat the pressure cooker. Add the oil and saute the onion until it is translucent. Stir in the remaining ingredients except the shrimp and tomato paste.

2. Secure the cover and make sure the pressure gauge is in place. Bring the cooker to pressure according to the instructions that accompany your individual pressure cooker, then time the cooker for 1 minute.

8 servings
Serving size: 1/8 recipe
Vegetable Exchange..........2
Lean Meat Exchange.......2
Calories............................171
Total Fat.........................6 g
   Calories from Fat......51
Cholesterol................94 mg
Sodium.....................321 mg
Carbohydrate...............10 g
   Dietary Fiber..............2 g
Protein...........................19 g

3. Reduce pressure by placing the cooker under running water. When pressure is down, remove the lid and gently stir in the tomato paste. Then add the frozen shrimp. Bring the gumbo to a boil. Serve when heated through.

Porcupine Meatballs

8 oz lean ground beef
1/3 cup white rice
1 1/2 Tbsp minced onion
1/4 tsp pepper
1/8 tsp paprika
1/8 tsp oregano
1 cup tomato sauce
1 1/2 cups water

1. Mix all ingredients except the tomato sauce and water until well blended. Form into 6 meatballs. Place the rack in the pressure cooker. Pour the tomato sauce and water into the cooker. Place the meatballs on the rack.

2. Secure the cover and make sure the pressure gauge is in place. Bring the cooker to pressure according to the instructions that accompany your individual pressure cooker, then time the cooker for 12 minutes.

3. Remove the cooker from the heat and let the pressure drop of its own accord.

3 servings
Serving size: 2 meatballs
Starch Exchange................1
Vegetable Exchange..........1
Medium-Fat Meat
    Exchange........................2
Calories.........................244
Total Fat ....10 g
    Calories from Fat......90
Cholesterol ....47 mg
Sodium ....493 mg
Carbohydrate..............22 g
    Dietary Fiber ....1 g
Protein ....17 g

Chicken Jardiniere

Nonstick cooking spray
6 oz boneless, skinless chicken breast, cut into 1-inch cubes
1/2 tsp chicken bouillon granules
1/2 cup water
2 medium potatoes, quartered
2 carrots, cut in chunks
2 turnips, quartered
2 stalks celery, cut in chunks
1 medium onion, quartered

1. Spray the pressure cooker pan with nonstick cooking spray. Brown the chicken evenly on all sides in the cooker. In a small bowl, dissolve the bouillon granules in the water.

2. Remove the chicken, put the rack in the cooker, and place the chicken and vegetables on the rack. Pour the bouillon over the ingredients.

3. Secure the cover and make sure the pressure gauge is in place. Bring the cooker to pressure according to the instructions that accompany your individual pressure cooker, then time the cooker for 4 minutes. Cool the pressure cooker immediately under cold running water.

2 servings
Serving size: 1/2 recipe
Starch Exchange 2
Vegetable Exchange...........1
Lean Meat Exchange 2
Calories 260
Total Fat ....4 g
    Calories from Fat......36
Cholesterol...............48 mg
Sodium ....362 mg
Carbohydrate ....33 g
    Dietary Fiber.............6 g
Protein.......................22 g

Apple Crumble

4 cups sliced Yellow Delicious apples
1 Tbsp lemon juice
1 cup quick-cooking oats
1/3 cup flour
1 tsp cinnamon
1/2 tsp salt
1/4 cup low-calorie margarine, melted
Nonstick cooking spray
2 cups water

1. Sprinkle the apples with the lemon juice. In a separate bowl, combine the oats, flour, cinnamon, salt, and margarine. Spray nonstick cooking spray into a metal bowl that will fit loosely into the cooker.

2. Place alternate layers of apples and oat mixture in the bowl, beginning and ending with apples. Cover the bowl tightly with aluminum foil and place on the rack in the cooker. Add the water to the cooker.

6 servings
Serving size: 1/2 cup
Starch Exchange..............1
Fruit Exchange..................1
Fat Exchange 1
Calories...........................171
Total Fat ....7 g
 Calories from Fat......63
Cholesterol ....0 mg
Sodium ....229 mg
Carbohydrate ....26 g
 Dietary Fiber............3 g
Protein ....3 g

3. Secure the cover and make sure the pressure gauge is in place. Bring the cooker to pressure according to the instructions that accompany your individual pressure cooker, then time the cooker for 20 minutes. Cool the pressure cooker immediately under cold running water.

Grill of a Lifetime

Here are tips to make your barbecue healthy as well as hearty.

For Best Barbecue Flavor

- Marinate meats overnight for increased tenderness.
- Brush meats and poultry with fresh marinade or barbecue sauce before grilling and once or twice during the grilling for better flavor and color. (Be sure to wear insulated mitts and use a marinade brush.)
- Clean the grill with a stiff wire brush after each use. Black residue on the grill will make the food taste bitter and will carry over the flavor of the last meal.
- Don't put the food on the grill before the flame dies down. If the flame is too hot, the food will be charred, not cooked. When coals turn white, you know they are ready for cooking.
- Turn poultry or meat with tongs. Make sure they have long safety handles. Piercing meat or poultry with a fork lets some of the juices run out, which decreases the flavor.
- Flip the hamburgers and serve them with a spatula to help them keep their shape.
- Wrap fish in foil, or place it in the special metal holders available so it doesn't fall apart when you turn it or remove it from the grill.
- Consider buying a meat thermometer so you know when the large pieces of meat are barbecued to the correct temperature.

Keep it Fresh

- Eat first, then play. Bacteria grow more quickly the longer food sits in the heat.
- Avoid foods that pose high risks for food poisoning, such as salads with eggs in them or foods made with dairy products.

Great Grilling

- Make sure meat, poultry, and fish are not handled by more than one person, as this increases the risk of spreading bacteria to the food.
- Add mayonnaise or salad dressing to cold salads when the food is prepared, not just before eating. Contrary to popular belief, mayonnaise actually slows microbe growth in food.
- If you keep your food in a cooler, make sure each item is chilled by putting ice directly on top of it. Try to minimize the number of times you open the cooler, because each opening lets cold air out. Keep your cooler in a shaded area.
- Don't place cooked food back onto the same plate that held raw meat, fish, or poultry. The cooked product could become contaminated with bacteria from the raw food that was previously on the plate.
- Don't taste a meat product to check for doneness. Eating even a little bit of undercooked meat could cause problems if the harmful bacteria in it are still alive.

Make it Nutritious!

- Use poultry and fish more often than red meats.
- Use low-fat cuts of beef and pork, such as beef round, sirloin, flank steak and tenderloin, pork tenderloin, fresh ham, or veal chops.
- Buy ground beef that's extra lean, with less than 15 percent fat. Ask the butcher to grind the beef from low-fat cuts, such as top round.
- Keep in mind that most hot dogs are high-fat products.
- Trim all excess fat from meat and poultry before cooking them.
- Serve plenty of fresh vegetables and fruits at your barbecue.
- If you do use mayonnaise or dressings, make sure they are low in fat and calories.
- Substitute plain nonfat yogurt for sour cream on salads or baked potatoes.

Stay Safe!

- Take care to anchor the grill securely, making sure it will not tip over if accidentally bumped.
- Be sure the cooking surface is flat and level.
- Keep children and pets from running around near the grill. Accidents can happen quickly.
- Never leave a baby, young child, or pet alone in the yard—even for a minute—when the grill is lit or is still hot. Bring out all the food (under ice in the cooler), dishes, and other supplies before you heat up the grill so you won't have to run back into the house or car and risk leaving children alone with the heated grill. If you have a portable phone, bring that out of the house as well so you won't have to leave the yard to answer the phone.
- Be sure to light a charcoal grill only with a commercial fire starter. Don't use gasoline or alcohol.
- Avoid fire flare-ups—in addition to being a fire hazard, burning juice or fat can produce smoke that may be harmful.
- Wear over-the-wrist, insulated cooking mitts when you are working near the barbecue. It's easy to touch something hot accidentally and get a painful burn.
- Keeping a first-aid kit nearby, especially one that will let you care for burns, is a smart precaution.

Grilled Vegetable Delight

Butter-flavored nonstick cooking spray
2 medium tomatoes, cored
1 cup fresh mushrooms, sliced
1 medium onion, sliced
1 small zucchini, sliced
1 oz mozzarella cheese

1. Spray 2 pieces of aluminum foil lightly with nonstick cooking spray. Put half the vegetables on each foil piece and sprinkle with the cheese.

2. Close each foil packet and grill for 10–15 minutes. Carefully open packet to serve.

2 servings
Serving size: 1/2 recipe
Vegetable Exchange..........2
Medium-Fat Meat
    Exchange 1/2
Calories 93
Total Fat ....1 g
    Calories from Fat.........9
Cholesterol...................4 mg
Sodium ....51 mg
Carbohydrate...............15 g
    Dietary Fiber..............4 g
Protein ....5 g

Grilled Potatoes

Butter-flavored nonstick cooking spray
2 medium raw potatoes, sliced thin
1/2 onion, sliced
2 Tbsp chopped mushrooms
1/8 cup chopped green pepper

Spray aluminum foil lightly with nonstick cooking spray. Put all ingredients in foil. Close tightly and grill for 1 hour, turning frequently.

4 servings
Serving size: 1/4 recipe
Starch Exchange.................1
Vegetable Exchange...........1
Calories 114
Total Fat.........................0 g
    Calories from Fat.........0
Cholesterol ....0 mg
Sodium.........................9 mg
Carbohydrate..............25 g
    Dietary Fiber..............3 g
Protein ....3 g

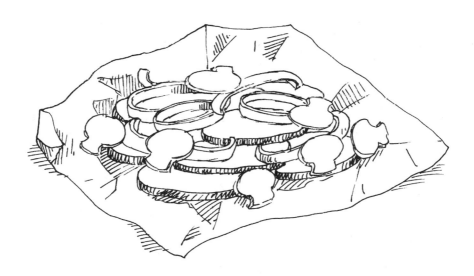

Grilled Picante Chicken

1 cup picante sauce
4 tsp sugar substitute
4 tsp Dijon mustard
2 lb boneless, skinless chicken breast

1. Combine the picante sauce, sugar substitute, and mustard, and marinate the chicken breast in this mixture in the refrigerator for 4–8 hours.

2. Grill the chicken breast for 10–15 minutes, turning once, until well done.

8 servings
Serving size: 4 oz
Lean Meat Exchange 4
Calories............................154
Total Fat.........................3 g
  Calories from Fat.......27
Cholesterol ....73 mg
Sodium ....217 mg
Carbohydrate ....3 g
  Dietary Fiber..............0 g
Protein...........................27 g

Luscious Leftovers

You can make delicious meals from leftover poultry! Leftovers not only provide the basis for new dishes, but extend others. Chunks of turkey or chicken add flavor, protein, and substance to vegetable or pasta salads, soups, and casseroles.

How to make sure you'll have those valuable leftovers? Simple. Buy more than you need for one dinner. Buy an extra-large turkey for the holidays, or roast an extra breast at the same time as your bird.

Make sure you store leftover turkey carefully. Bacteria can multiply rapidly if high-protein foods, like poultry, aren't handled correctly. As soon as the meal is finished, divide the leftovers into small portions and refrigerate them in small, shallow, covered containers. This allows them to cool adequately. Cooked turkey or chicken will keep 3–4 days in the refrigerator.

Or, you can freeze the diced or shredded leftover poultry after wrapping it well. You can also freeze most of the foods you make from leftovers. Wrap such foods securely in aluminum foil or freezer bags, or place them in tightly closed plastic containers. Label the package or container with the date and the contents. It's best to use the frozen leftovers within one or two months for best quality.

Try being creative with leftover turkey in the following recipes.

South-of-the-Border Turkey Pitas

6 small whole-wheat pita breads
2 cups cooked turkey, shredded
1/2 cup chopped onion
1 pkg (1 1/4 oz) taco seasoning mix
1 cup water
1/2 cup plain nonfat yogurt
1/4 cup salsa
1/4 tsp cumin
1/4 tsp chili powder
1 cup shredded lettuce

1. Preheat the oven to 350°F. Wrap the pita bread in aluminum foil. Place the turkey, onion, taco seasoning, and water in a saucepan. Heat over medium heat, stirring occasionally, until the mixture comes to a boil. Lower the heat and simmer for 15 minutes.

2. Heat the wrapped pita bread in the oven for 10 minutes or until it is warm and pliable. Meanwhile, combine the yogurt, salsa, cumin, and chili powder in a small bowl. Take the pita bread out of the oven and unwrap. Split each bread to make a pocket.

3. Spread the inside of each pita pocket with 1 Tbsp of the salsa mixture. Divide the turkey mixture evenly into each pita pocket. Sprinkle on the shredded lettuce and top with an additional Tbsp of the salsa mixture.

6 servings
Serving size: 1/6 recipe
Starch Exchange...............1
Lean Meat Exchange.......2
Calories 190
Total Fat.......................3 g
    Calories from Fat.......27
Cholesterol ....36 mg
Sodium....................588 mg
Carbohydrate...............22 g
    Dietary Fiber.............0 g
Protein...........................19 g

Luscious Leftovers

Turkey Gumbo Soup

3 cups low-fat, low-sodium chicken broth
1 cup cooked turkey, diced
1/2 cup chopped onion
1/4 cup chopped celery
1 10-oz pkg frozen cut okra
1 16-oz can tomatoes
1/2 tsp salt
1/8 tsp pepper
1/4 cup white rice

1. Heat the chicken broth to boiling in a large stockpot, then add all remaining ingredients.

2. Cover and let boil gently for 20 minutes until the vegetables and rice are tender.

6 servings
Serving size: 1 cup
Starch Exchange................1
Lean Meat Exchange.....1/2
Calories...........................102
Total Fat ....2 g
    Calories from Fat 18
Cholesterol.................13 mg
Sodium...................320 mg
Carbohydrate...............15 g
    Dictary Fiber ....1 g
Protein............................7 g

Wild Rice Soup

3 Tbsp low-calorie margarine
1/2 cup diced onion
1/2 cup chopped celery
3 Tbsp flour
1/2 tsp salt
1/4 tsp pepper
2 cups low-fat, low-sodium chicken broth
1 cup skim milk
1 1/2 cups cooked wild rice (may substitute white rice)
1 cup cooked turkey, diced

1. Melt the margarine in a skillet over low heat. Saute the onion and celery until tender-crisp, about 2–3 minutes. Stir in the flour, salt, and pepper.

2. Add the chicken broth and milk, and stir over medium heat until thickened. Add the wild rice and turkey, and heat to serving temperature.

6 servings
Serving size: 1 cup
Starch Exchange...............1
Medium-Fat Meat
    Exchange........................1
Calories............................154
Total Fat...........................5 g
   Calories from Fat......45
Cholesterol................19 mg
Sodium.....................310 mg
Carbohydrate...............19 g
   Dietary Fiber.............0 g
Protein.............................9 g

Barbecued Turkey Sandwiches

3 Tbsp instant minced onion
1/4 cup plus 2 Tbsp catsup
3 Tbsp vinegar
1 tsp salt
2 Tbsp sugar
1 1/2 tsp Worcestershire sauce
1 1/2 tsp prepared mustard
1/4 tsp pepper
1/2 tsp paprika
2 cups cooked turkey, diced
6 hamburger buns

1. In a small mixing bowl, combine all ingredients except the turkey and hamburger buns; mix well.

2. Place the mixture in a saucepan. Add turkey and bring to a boil over medium heat. Reduce the heat, cover, and simmer for 15–20 minutes.

3. Serve the hot barbecued turkey on the hamburger buns.

6 servings
Serving size: 1/2 cup
Starch Exchange............1/2
Lean Meat Exchange 2
Calories 121
Total Fat ....2 g
　　Calories from Fat 18
Cholesterol................34 mg
Sodium.....................590 mg
Carbohydrate................10 g
　　Dietary Fiber..............0 g
Protein.............................15 g

Cooking for One or Two

If the thought of preparing a meal for one makes you wonder whether it's worth it, you've got company. Many people—single, divorced, widowed, working or retired, noncooks, and homemakers—face solo meals morning and night.

Yet eating well is important to everyone, particularly people with diabetes. Don't fall into the "why bother?" syndrome. You're worth cooking for—and it doesn't have to take all day! Try some of the following tips, and the recipes below, to make special meals for yourself.

■ Arrange a pleasant table setting, pick a colorful place-mat, and brighten your condiment arrangement with a pretty salt and pepper shaker set. Try cheery live or artificial flowers. Then take the trouble to prepare something you'd serve a guest.

■ Try establishing a schedule. The body responds to routine, and if you get used to eating at a certain time, you'll start feeling hungry at that time. A regular mealtime will encourage you to prepare food ahead, and hunger will help bring mealtime satisfaction.

■ Let the odor of food preparations waft through the house. The smell of cooking food can do a lot to wake up a poor appetite.

■ Inviting someone to eat with you is a good way to ensure that you'll prepare a proper meal. Think about making a special dinner and invite a colleague, a neighbor, or a relative you rarely see.

■ Keep variety in your diet. When you eat alone, it's easy to prepare one or two items over and over, like a peanut butter sandwich or a can of soup. But a healthy diet is a varied diet. Remember the side dishes—salads, vegetables, fruit, milk, or juice.

- Remember that canned foods are usually high in salt. So check the sodium content on labels, and look for low-sodium products.
- Invest in a microwave. It's easy and it's fast.
- Make up a menu. Before going to bed, write down your next day's meals. Planning makes a difference.
- Remember fresh foods when you shop. They're generally more economical and healthier than packaged or pre-cooked products, and they often need only minimal preparation.
- Cook ahead of time. Prepare an entire recipe when you have time or feel like it, then freeze it in portions you can easily remove and heat.
- Look for simple cooking ideas. For instance, microwave a skinless turkey or chicken breast for 10 to 15 minutes, then drizzle it with tangy or spicy tomato sauce. Or open a can of vegetable, navy, or kidney bean soup and add 2 ounces of dry pasta. Microwave or boil together for 10 minutes, and you have a meal for 2 days.
- You can also mix 1 cup of rice; 3 ounces of chopped, uncooked, skinned chicken breast; 1 cup of frozen broccoli; and 3 cups of purchased or homemade low-fat chicken or vegetable stock (skimmed of fat). Boil together for 20 to 25 minutes, and let stand for a few minutes so the rice absorbs the liquid. You'll have a delicious, healthy dinner for 3 nights.

Fettucine with Cream Sauce

2 oz uncooked spinach fettucine
2 Tbsp 1% cottage cheese
2 Tbsp part-skim ricotta cheese
2 tsp nonfat buttermilk
1 tsp Parmesan cheese
1/4 small tomato, finely chopped
1/2 tsp parsley flakes

1. Cook the fettucine in boiling water, uncovered, for 9–12 minutes. Process the cheeses and buttermilk in a blender or food processor until smooth.

2. Heat the cheese mixture in a double boiler or microwave oven. Add the Parmesan cheese and stir. Add the tomato and parsley flakes; stir.

3. Spoon the sauce over the hot fettucine and toss. Serve immediately.

1 serving
Serving size: 1 cup
Starch Exchange 2
Lean Meat Exchange 1
Calories..........................235
Total Fat ....4 g
    Calories from Fat......36
Cholesterol................113 mg
Sodium......................201 mg
Carbohydrate...............32 g
Protein..........................13 g

Easy Meat Loaf Balls

Nonstick cooking spray
4 oz lean ground beef
1/8 tsp garlic powder
1/8 tsp Italian seasoning
1 oz canned mushroom stems and pieces, drained
1 egg white
2 Tbsp oat bran or 2 crushed wheat-type crackers
2 Tbsp tomato sauce or catsup

1. Preheat the oven to 350°F. Lightly coat a small (4 x 6-inch) muffin tin with nonstick cooking spray. Combine all ingredients except the tomato sauce or catsup. Shape into 2 balls.

2. Place each ball in a muffin compartment. Top each ball with 1 Tbsp of tomato sauce or catsup. Bake for 15–20 minutes. Drain the meatballs on a paper towel before serving.

2 servings
Serving size: 1 meatball
Vegetable Exchange...........1
Medium-Fat Meat
    Exchange.......................2
Calories............................185
Total Fat.........................11 g
    Calories from Fat......99
Cholesterol................50 mg
Sodium ....282 mg
Carbohydrate ....4 g
Protein ....18 g

Light Spinach Salad

4 cups fresh spinach, torn
4 oz boneless, skinless, cooked chicken breast, cubed
4 medium oranges, peeled and sectioned
1/2 cup sliced fresh mushrooms
1 small onion, sliced
2 oz low-fat cheese, cubed or in strips
2 Tbsp any low-calorie dressing

Combine all ingredients except the cheese and dressing in a large bowl; chill. Before serving, add the cheese and toss with dressing. (Dressing not included in nutrient analysis.)

2 servings
Serving size: 1/2 recipe
Fruit Exchange...................2
Vegetable Exchange..........2
Lean Meat Exchange.......3
Calories 355
Total Fat........................9 g
   Calories from Fat 81
Cholesterol ....65 mg
Sodium....................383 mg
Carbohydrate...............41 g
Protein...........................27 g

Bean Soup

1 can vegetarian soup
1 1/2 cups water
1 cup canned kidney beans
1 cup shell pasta
1 tsp chopped parsley
1/4 cup sliced zucchini
1/2 tsp basil
1/4 tsp marjoram
1/2 tsp lite soy sauce

Put all ingredients in a medium saucepan and cook over medium heat until the pasta is tender, about 8 minutes.

3 servings
Serving size: 1 cup
Starch Exchange 2
Vegetable Exchange..........2
Calories..........................207
Total Fat....................1 1/2 g
    Calories from Fat........13
Cholesterol ....0 mg
Sodium ....581 mg
Carbohydrate ....40 g
Protein............................9 g

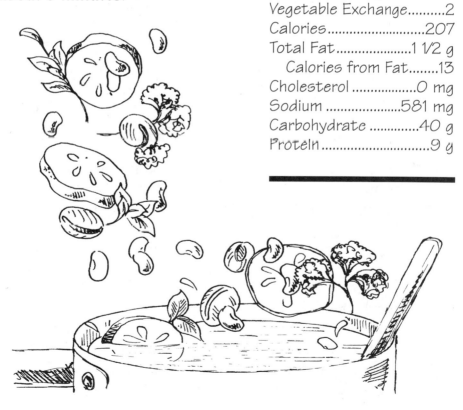

From You, with Love

Looking for a different kind of gift for a friend or family member? Give the best, something of yourself: a gift you have made and packaged for a special friend. Although you can create many items out of fabric, paper, wood, or clay, homemade foods carry a touch of family and home, the scent of the holiday kitchen, and a memory of happy times to recall the rest of the year.

They are also fun to make, attractive to give, and often one of the most welcome, yet least expensive, gifts you can offer. Your food present will be even more welcome and useful if you tailor it to the recipient's dietary needs, then enclose recipes or serving suggestions for its use. If your friend has diabetes or is watching his or her weight, include the nutrient analysis information on a pretty gift card.

You might also combine your food gift with something for the kitchen, such as a wooden spoon, cutting board, grater, or trivet. The package, too, can be useful—a basket, casserole dish, baking pan, or storage container.

While you're letting your imagination roam, keep your mind on your time schedule. Many additional activities crowd the holiday hours, so plan ahead. Prepare food items early and freeze them, if appropriate. If you are going to make special packaging, remember you may need time to find necessary items, with a day or so for glue or paint to dry.

You'll need airtight containers to store most food gifts and shakers with lids for others. So save salad dressing bottles, margarine or whipped topping tubs, snack and coffee cans with plastic lids, large glass jars and baby food jars with screw lids, spice jars with shaker tops (plastic or glass), unusual salt or pepper shakers, and tins that held popcorn or other snacks. You might place a variety of small items or a handful of snacks in a pretty stationery or jewelry box, or a never-used flower pot or vase. Don't forget to hold onto pretty or unusual wrapping paper and ribbons, too.

Soak appropriate containers 30 to 60 minutes in hot, soapy water to get them thoroughly clean and to remove all labels. Then, if you wish, paint or cover them with contact paper, or personalize them with stickers, decals, paste- or paint-on initials, wallpaper, or colored ribbons. You can put as many servings as you wish into each container.

An easy way to start is by making a Bouquet Garni. Simply measure out 1 Tbsp parsley, 1 tsp basil, 1 tsp rosemary, 1 tsp oregano, 2 bay leaves, 6 whole peppercorns, and 1 clove garlic. Place all the ingredients together and divide into four parts. Put each part in a piece of cheesecloth. Secure the top by tying with a piece of string.

To use the Bouquet Garni, add one packet to soups or stews for seasoning. Put the packet into the liquid, leaving the string hanging out. Then remove the Bouquet Garni before serving. Discard after use.

Or try this Poultry Seasoning mix: combine 2 cups dried parsley, 1 cup ground sage, 1/2 cup dried rosemary (crushed), 1/2 cup dried marjoram (crushed), 3 Tbsp salt, 1 Tbsp pepper, 2 tsp onion powder, and 1/2 tsp ginger. Add a note to shake the mixture well before using.

Buttermilk Dressing Mix

1 cup buttermilk powder or nonfat powdered milk
4 tsp dried basil, crushed
4 tsp minced dried onion
2 tsp dry mustard
1 tsp garlic powder
1/2 tsp salt

1. Combine all ingredients and stir well. Divide into four parts, and store in airtight containers.

2. To use, combine 1 packet (1/4 cup of mix) with 1/2 cup water. Blend into 3/4 cup nonfat yogurt. Shake well before using.

3. Each packet, combined with yogurt and water, makes 1 1/2 cups of dressing.

12 servings
Serving size: 2 Tbsp
Free Food
Calories 18
Total Fat.........................0 g
    Calories from Fat.........0
Cholesterol...................2 mg
Sodium......................46 mg
Carbohydrate.................2 g
Protein ....2 g

Apple Butter

5 lb apples (try Pippin, Granny Smith, or Macintosh)
2 cups water
1 cup orange juice
2 cups unsweetened apple cider
2 tsp cinnamon
1 tsp cloves
1 tsp allspice
1/2 tsp nutmeg

1. Peel, core, and thinly slice apples. Put the apples, water, orange juice, and apple cider in a saucepan and simmer for 20–25 minutes. Remove from heat and puree the apple and liquid in a food processor or blender until the mixture is fairly smooth.

96 servings
Serving size: 1 Tbsp
Free Food
Calories 17
Total Fat.........................0 g
    Calories from Fat.........0
Carbohydrate ....4 g
Protein...........................0 g

2. Preheat the oven to 325°F.
    Pour the apple mixture into a large baking pan and bake, uncovered, for about 1 hour, or until reduced to half. Stir occasionally. (It's best to have a baking pan with a large surface so the moisture can evaporate.)

3. Add the spices and stir to blend. Lower the oven temperature to 250°F and bake the mixture for 3 hours until very dark and thick. Stir frequently to prevent sticking. Place in hot, sterilized Mason jars. Cool and store in refrigerator.

Recipes from around the World

Tomato, Pepper, and Sausage Appetizer

1 tsp canola oil
1 1/2 cups finely chopped onion
1/2 tsp finely chopped garlic
2 Tbsp Hungarian paprika (available in large supermarkets)
3 medium green peppers, seeded and cut into 1/2-inch strips
2 medium red peppers, seeded and cut into 1/2-inch strips
1 1/2 cups tomatoes, peeled, seeded, and finely chopped
1/2 tsp salt
Fresh ground pepper to taste
1/2 cup tomato puree
3 oz sausage, cut into thin slices

1. Heat the oil in a 2-qt saucepan. Add the onion and garlic, and saute over low heat for 7–10 minutes. Remove from heat and stir in the paprika.

2. Add the green and red pepper strips, tomatoes, salt, and pepper. If the vegetables are not completely covered, add enough of the tomato puree to cover them. Cover the saucepan and return to medium heat. Let simmer for 10 minutes.

6 servings
Serving size: 1 cup
Starch Exchange................1
Fat Exchange 1
Calories 125
Total Fat..........................6 g
    Saturated Fat...........2 g
    Calories from Fat 53
Cholesterol................10 mg
Sodium ....564 mg
Carbohydrate...............16 g
    Dietary Fiber..............4 g
    Sugars ....8 g
Protein ....4 g

3. Add the rest of the tomato puree and the sliced sausage. Cover, turn the heat to low, and allow the mixture to simmer for another 1/2 hour. (The finished appetizer should have the consistency of tomato sauce.)

Hungarian Goulash

1 Tbsp vegetable oil
1 cup coarsely chopped onion
3 tsp paprika
1 lb lean stewing beef, trimmed and cut into 3/4-inch cubes
1 1/2 cups water
3 Tbsp low-fat, low-sodium beef broth
1/4 tsp salt
1/2 tsp marjoram
2 medium green peppers, seeded and cut into 1/2-inch strips
2 cups small peeled tomatoes, fresh or canned
1/4 tsp caraway seeds, crushed with the back of a spoon

1. Heat the oil in a stockpot. Saute the onion and paprika for 3 minutes. Add the meat cubes and brown for 5–6 minutes, turning to brown on all sides. Add the water, broth, salt, and marjoram to the stockpot and stir well, scraping up all the drippings from the bottom of the pot and mixing with the liquid.

2. Make sure the meat is covered with liquid. If not, add more water. Cover the stockpot and simmer the goulash for 1 hour over low heat. Add more water as needed to keep meat covered. After 1 hour, add the green pepper strips and tomatoes. Cover and continue simmering for 7–10 more minutes, stirring occasionally. Garnish with caraway seeds and serve.

5 servings
Serving size: 1 cup
Vegetable Exchange...........2
Lean Meat Exchange 2
Fat Exchange...................1/2
Calories............................184
Total Fat.........................8 g
  Saturated Fat............2 g
  Calories from Fat......68
Cholesterol................49 mg
Sodium ....318 mg
Carbohydrate ....12 g
  Dietary Fiber ....2 g
  Sugars........................6 g
Protein ....18 g

Potato Dumplings

5 medium potatoes (about 1 1/2 lb)
1 tsp salt
1/3 cup flour
1 egg, lightly beaten
2 tsp milk
1/4 cup flour

1. Peel the potatoes, then boil them until they are very soft, about 40 minutes. Let the potatoes cool, then put them through a ricer or finely dice them. In a mixing bowl, combine the potatoes, salt, 1/3 cup flour, egg, and milk. Mix with a wooden spoon (a wooden spoon helps develop the gluten in the flour) until you have a smooth paste.

6 servings
Serving size: 2 dumplings
Starch Exchange 1 1/2
Calories 134
Total Fat ....1 g
   Saturated Fat...........0 g
   Calories from Fat 10
Cholesterol ....36 mg
Sodium ....404 mg
Carbohydrate ....27 g
   Dietary Fiber ....2 g
   Sugars ....2 g
Protein ....4 g

2. Use the 1/4 cup flour to dust your hands to keep them from getting sticky as you work. Form the mixture into 12 1-inch dumpling balls. Drop 6 dumplings into 5 quarts of boiling water. Let the water come back to a gentle boil. Don't stir the water while the dumplings are in it.

3. When the dumplings rise to the surface of the water, they are done. Remove them with a slotted spoon and place them on a plate. Continue with the next 6 dumplings. Serve with goulash or roasted chicken.

Hungary

Red Beet Salad

1 16-oz can beets, julienned (reserve juice)
1/4 tsp caraway seeds
1 tsp red (mild) or white (strong) horseradish
2 Tbsp white vinegar
1/2 tsp sugar

Combine all ingredients, mix lightly, cover, and chill for 2 hours. Drain off the liquid before serving.

5 servings
Serving size: 1/2 cup
Vegetable Exchange............1
Calories 28
Total Fat.........................0 g
   Saturated Fat...........0 g
   Calories from Fat 1
Cholesterol ....0 mg
Sodium ....234 mg
Carbohydrate.................7 g
   Dietary Fiber ....1 g
   Sugars ....4 g
Protein ....1 g

Hungary

Mushroom Appetizer

2 Tbsp corn or sunflower oil
2 cups diced onion
1/2 cup diced garlic
1 cup chopped parsley
1/2 cup diced green onion
4 lb mushrooms, cleaned and finely diced
3 Tbsp Worcestershire sauce
1/4 tsp hot pepper sauce
1/4 tsp lemon juice (plus a few drops to sprinkle on top)
1/4 tsp salt
1/2 tsp pepper
1/4 tsp paprika
2 bunches fresh watercress, chopped

1. Heat the oil in a large skillet. Saute the onion, garlic, and parsley for 2–3 minutes, then add the green onion and mushrooms and saute for 5–6 more minutes.

2. Add the remaining ingredients and stir well. Sprinkle with lemon juice. Serve hot or cold, over melba toast rounds or pita wedges.

16 servings
Serving size: 1/3 cup
Vegetable Exchange..........2
Calories.............................60
Total Fat..........................2 g
    Calories from Fat.......18
Cholesterol..................0 mg
Sodium......................70 mg
Carbohydrate................9 g
    Dietary Fiber.............2 g
Protein............................3 g

Connecticut Mohegan Succotash

2 Tbsp corn or sunflower oil
1 cup diced green onion
1 green pepper, cut into slim cubes or triangles
1/4 cup diced garlic
3 cups water or low-fat, low-sodium chicken broth
2 32-oz pkg frozen corn
2 32-oz pkg frozen baby lima beans
1 medium yellow squash, cubed
1 medium zucchini, cubed
1 tsp pepper
1/4 tsp paprika
1/4 tsp salt
1/4 cup chopped green onion
1/2 cup chopped parsley

1. In a large skillet or saucepan, heat the oil and saute the green onion, pepper, and garlic for 3 minutes, stirring well. Add the water or chicken broth, corn, lima beans, and squash. Slowly bring the mixture to a simmering boil, stirring occasionally.

2. Season with the pepper, paprika, and salt. Cover, reduce heat, and simmer the mixture for another 10–15 minutes, stirring once. Garnish with green onion and parsley, or stir them into the mixture, then allow the succotash to sit, covered, for 5 minutes before serving.

16 servings
Serving size: 1/2 cup
Starch Exchange 3
Calories...........................216
Total Fat........................3 g
    Calories from Fat.......27
Cholesterol ....0 mg
Sodium......................99 mg
Carbohydrate..............42 g
    Dietary Fiber..............8 g
Protein ....10 g

Pathfinder Bread

1 1/2–2 cups white flour
1/2 cup yellow cornmeal
1/2 cup buckwheat flour
1 pkg dry yeast
3/4 tsp salt

3 Tbsp margarine
1 cup boiling water
1/4 cup light molasses
Nonstick cooking spray

1. Preheat the oven to 350°F. Place half the white flour into a bowl. Add the cornmeal, buckwheat flour, yeast, and salt. In another bowl, combine the margarine with the boiling water, stirring until the margarine is melted. Add the molasses. Combine the flour mixture with the molasses and margarine; dough will be sticky.

14 servings
Serving size: 1 slice
Starch Exchange 2
Calories...........................140
Total Fat..........................3 g
    Calories from Fat.......27
Cholesterol ....0 mg
Sodium ....136 mg
Carbohydrate ....26 g
    Dietary Fiber ....2 g
Protein ....3 g

2. Knead the dough for 8–10 minutes on a wooden board rubbed with flour. Knead until dough is no longer very sticky, adding flour if necessary. Spray a large bowl with nonstick cooking spray, add the dough, and turn it so that all sides are lightly coated. Cover with an inverted bowl and let the dough rise in a warm place until it nearly doubles in size, about 1–1 1/2 hours.

3. Punch the dough down and knead it again, briefly. Shape it into an oblong loaf. Spray an oblong bread pan with nonstick cooking spray. Place punched-down dough in the pan, cover, and let rise again for about 1 hour, or until doubled in volume. Bake for 45–50 minutes until the bread sounds hollow when tapped and is a deep brown color.

Barley Soup

1 Tbsp olive oil
1/2 cup chopped onion
1 medium carrot, washed, peeled, and diced
8 cups water
1 low-sodium beef bouillon cube
1/2 tsp pepper
1/4 cup pearl barley
1/4 cup lentils
2 Tbsp long-grain white rice
1 cup chopped Italian or flat parsley
1 Tbsp lemon juice

1. Heat the olive oil in a large saucepan and saute the onion and carrot for 5 minutes.

2. Add the water, bouillon cube, and pepper. Bring to a boil, then add the barley, lentils, and rice. Let cook for 45 minutes over low heat.

3. Add the parsley and cook 30 minutes more. Add the lemon juice before serving.

6 servings
Serving size: 1 cup
Starch Exchange.................1
Fat Exchange...................1/2
Calories 109
Total Fat..........................3 g
   Saturated Fat ....1/2 g
   Calories from Fat.......27
Cholesterol ....0 mg
Sodium ....16 mg
Carbohydrate..............18 g
   Dietary Fiber ....3 g
   Sugars ....3 g
Protein............................0 g

Chicken Kabob

1 lb boneless, skinless chicken breast
1/2 tsp salt
1/2 tsp pepper
1/4 tsp saffron or turmeric
1 cup fresh lemon or lime juice
2 cloves garlic, chopped
1/2 cup chopped onion

1. Cut the chicken into 16 pieces. Place in a medium bowl and season with salt and pepper. Dissolve the saffron or turmeric in the lemon or lime juice, then add the garlic and onion to the juice mixture.

2. Pour the juice mixture over the chicken, cover the bowl, and marinate in the refrigerator for at least 12 hours.

3. Thread the chicken pieces onto 4 skewers. Grill or broil the chicken skewers for 6–8 minutes on each side until well cooked.

4 servings
Serving size: 4 oz
Lean Meat Exchange.......3
Calories...........................140
Total Fat.........................3 g
   Saturated Fat............1 g
   Calories from Fat.......27
Cholesterol...............68 mg
Sodium.....................199 mg
Carbohydrate.................2 g
   Dietary Fiber..............0 g
   Sugars........................2 g
Protein...........................25 g

Lentil Salad

2 cups lentils
7 cups water
1/4 cup chopped onion
1 low-sodium beef bouillon cube
1 tsp cumin
2 Tbsp olive oil
1/4 cup fresh lemon or lime juice
1/2 tsp pepper
2 Tbsp minced mint or flat leaf parsley

1. Wash the lentils and remove any discolored lentils. Place the lentils in a large saucepan or stockpot with the water, onion, bouillon, and cumin.

2. Bring to a boil, then reduce the heat to low. Cover and let simmer for about 45 minutes. Lentils are cooked when they are soft. Drain remaining liquid. Place the cooked lentils in the refrigerator to cool for at least 1 hour.

3. In a small bowl, combine the oil, juice, and pepper. Pour over the cooked lentils and add the mint or parsley. Toss to mix. Serve lentils at room temperature.

6 servings
Serving size: 1 cup
Starch Exchange........2 1/2
Very Lean Meat
    Exchange.........................2
Calories 263
Total Fat.........................5 g
    Saturated Fat............1 g
    Calories from Fat......46
Cholesterol ....0 mg
Sodium ....7 mg
Carbohydrate ....38 g
    Dietary Fiber...........20 g
    Sugars ....4 g
Protein ....18 g

Persia

Fisch Rouladen

1 1/2 lb filet of sole or flounder
2 Tbsp corn oil margarine
1/3 cup chopped onion
1/4 cup chopped celery
1/2 cup chopped mushrooms
2 Tbsp chopped parsley
1 Tbsp flour
Nonstick cooking spray
2 Tbsp Parmesan cheese
1 tsp paprika
1/4 cup low-fat, low-sodium chicken broth

1. Preheat the oven to 350°F. Cut the fish into 6 pieces. Heat the margarine in a medium skillet and saute the onion and celery for 5 minutes. Add the mushrooms and parsley and cook for 5 more minutes, stirring to mix thoroughly.

2. Spread 2 Tbsp of the vegetable mixture on each filet. Roll up each filet, fasten with toothpicks, then sprinkle with flour. Spray the rolled fish lightly with nonstick cooking spray.

6 servings
Serving size: 1 roulade
Lean Meat Exchange 3
Calories 160
Total Fat...........................6 g
    Calories from Fat 54
Cholesterol ....56 mg
Sodium ....174 mg
Carbohydrate ....3 g
    Dietary Fiber..............0 g
Protein ....23 g

3. Spray a baking pan lightly with spray, place the fish in the pan, and sprinkle with Parmesan cheese and paprika. Pour the chicken broth around the fish filets. Bake uncovered for 25–30 minutes. Remove toothpicks before serving.

Horseradish Potatoes

1 1/2 lb potatoes, peeled and cut into chunks
2 tsp corn oil margarine
1/8 tsp pepper
1/2 cup plain nonfat yogurt
1 Tbsp horseradish, prepared
2 Tbsp chopped parsley

1. Boil the potatoes until tender, about 20–25 minutes. Drain and mash potatoes.

2. Add the remaining ingredients, whip lightly with a fork, and serve.

6 servings
Serving size: 1/2 cup
Starch Exchange...............1
Calories.............................88
Total Fat ....1 g
   Calories from Fat........ 9
Cholesterol ....0 mg
Sodium......................64 mg
Carbohydrate ....17 g
   Dietary Fiber ....1 g
Protein ....2 g

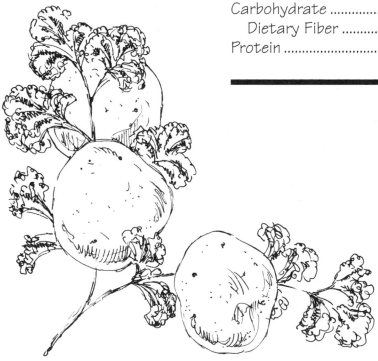

Red Cabbage

1 tsp corn oil margarine
1/3 cup chopped onion
4 cups red cabbage, shredded
1 cup cider vinegar
1/4 tsp cloves
1/4 cup apple juice
1/4 cup water
1 Tbsp flour
2 Tbsp sugar substitute

1. Melt the margarine in a large skillet and saute the onion until soft, about 5 minutes. Add the cabbage and stir to blend. Add the vinegar, cloves, apple juice, and water. Cook, covered, until the cabbage is tender, about 12 minutes.

2. In a cup, mix a small amount of the pan liquid with the flour. Add the flour mixture to the pan, stir, and simmer about 3–5 minutes, until the sauce thickens and is smooth. Stir in the sugar substitute and serve.

6 servings
Serving size: 1/2 cup
Vegetable Exchange...........1
Calories 34
Total Fat..........................0 g
    Calories from Fat.........0
Cholesterol ....0 mg
Sodium ....13 mg
Carbohydrate.................7 g
    Dietary Fiber.............0 g
Protein..............................0 g

Apple Bread Pudding

4 tsp unsalted margarine
4 slices white bread, cubed
4 medium apples, peeled and sliced
1/8 tsp cinnamon
1/8 tsp cloves
1/2 cup apple juice
1/3 cup raisins
1/2 tsp lemon zest
2 Tbsp lemon juice
2 Tbsp sugar substitute
Nonstick cooking spray

1. Preheat the oven to 325°F. Heat the margarine in a skillet over medium heat. Add the bread cubes and saute until lightly browned, about 3–5 minutes.

2. Combine the apple slices, cinnamon, cloves, apple juice, raisins, lemon zest, and lemon juice in a saucepan and simmer for 10 minutes, stirring occasionally. Remove from heat and add the sugar substitute.

6 servings
Serving size: 1/2 cup
Starch Exchange 2
Fat Exchange 1
Calories..........................148
Total Fat........................3 g
  Calories from Fat.......27
Cholesterol ....0 mg
Sodium.....................124 mg
Carbohydrate..............29 g
  Dietary Fiber..............3 g
Protein ....2 g

3. Spray a 2-qt baking dish with nonstick cooking spray. Alternate layers of bread cubes and apple mixture in the baking dish, starting and ending with bread cubes. Bake for 30 minutes.

Marinated Chicken Kabobs

1/8 cup canola oil
1/2 cup red wine vinegar
1/4 onion, sliced or diced
2 tsp rosemary
1/2 tsp salt
1/2 tsp pepper
2 lb boneless, skinless chicken breast, cut into 1-inch pieces
1 green pepper, cut into 1-inch pieces
1 onion, cut into 1-inch pieces
1 cup pineapple chunks, drained
24 mushrooms, cleaned
12 cherry tomatoes

1. Combine the oil, vinegar, onion, rosemary, salt, and pepper in a medium bowl. Cover and refrigerate for at least 2 hours. Add the chicken pieces and marinate in the refrigerator for at least 2 more hours.

2. To make the kabobs, alternate pieces of chicken, green pepper, onion, pineapple, and mushroom on 12 skewers. Add a cherry tomato at the top of each skewer. Grill or broil the kabobs for 6–8 minutes on each side until well done.

12 servings
Serving size: 1 kabob
Vegetable Exchange...........1
Lean Meat Exchange 2
Calories 152
Total Fat ....4 g
    Calories from Fat......36
Cholesterol................49 mg
Sodium.......................74 mg
Carbohydrate ....5 g
    Dietary Fiber ....1 g
Protein ....18 g

Wild Rice

1 Tbsp margarine
1 cup wild rice
1 1/2 cups sliced mushrooms
1/2 cup finely chopped green onion
2 1/4 cups water
1/4 cup dry white wine
1/4 tsp salt
1/4 tsp pepper
1 cup canned bamboo shoots

1. Melt the margarine in a 10-inch skillet. Add the wild rice, mushrooms, and onion. Saute over medium heat for 5 minutes, stirring frequently.

2. Stir in the water, wine, salt, and pepper. Heat to boiling, stirring occasionally; reduce heat. Cover and simmer until rice is tender, about 40–50 minutes.

3. Just before serving the rice, add bamboo shoots and continue cooking just until the bamboo shoots are heated through. If necessary, drain before serving.

8 servings
Serving size: 1/2 cup
Starch Exchange...............1
Vegetable Exchange...........1
Calories 100
Total Fat ....2 g
    Calories from Fat 18
Cholesterol ....0 mg
Sodium ....87 mg
Carbohydrate ....17 g
    Dietary Fiber..............6 g
Protein ....4 g

Hawaii

Gingered Broccoli

1/3 cup low-fat, low-sodium chicken broth
2 cloves garlic, minced fine
1 tsp grated fresh ginger root (peel before grating)
3 Tbsp lite soy sauce
1 Tbsp brown sugar
1 tsp canola oil
1 Tbsp cornstarch
2 Tbsp cold water
6 cups broccoli pieces, cooked

1. Heat the chicken broth in a wok or large skillet over medium heat. Add the garlic and ginger and stir for 1 minute. Add the soy sauce, brown sugar, and canola oil.

2. In a small bowl, combine the cornstarch and cold water and add to skillet. Continue cooking and stirring until the sauce thickens. Then add the broccoli and heat through.

6 servings
Serving size: 3/4 cup
Vegetable Exchange..........2
Calories 52
Total Fat ....1 g
 Calories from Fat.........9
Cholesterol ....0 mg
Sodium ....289 mg
Carbohydrate...............10 g
 Dietary Fiber.............4 g
Protein ....3 g

Island Fruit Cup

6 grapefruit sections
1/2 cup sliced fresh or canned pineapple
1/2 cup papaya (or cantaloupe or other melon)
1 medium orange, peeled and sectioned
1 medium banana
1/2 cup diced mango (or cantaloupe or other melon)
2 tsp sugar substitute
1 drop red food coloring (optional)
1/4 cup plain nonfat yogurt

1. Combine the fruits in a large bowl, then spoon into 6 individual serving dishes.

2. Blend the sugar substitute, food coloring, and yogurt. Top each serving with a dollop of yogurt. Serve well chilled.

6 servings
Serving size: 1/6 recipe
Fruit Exchange.....................1
Calories.............................66
Total Fat...........................0 g
    Calories from Fat.........0
Cholesterol ....0 mg
Sodium..........................8 mg
Carbohydrate...............16 g
    Dietary Fiber ....2 g
Protein ....1 g

Gazpacho Andaluz

3 lb medium tomatoes, diced
2 1/2 cups diced green pepper
1 cup diced onion
3 cups diced cucumbers
3 slices white bread, torn into pieces
2 cups cold water
5 Tbsp red wine vinegar
3 cloves garlic, minced
1 tsp salt
Sprigs of parsley

1. Set aside 1 cup tomatoes, 1/2 cup green pepper, 1/4 cup onion, and 1/2 cup cucumber in separate bowls; refrigerate. Combine the remaining tomato, green pepper, onion, and cucumber in one large bowl; add the bread and cold water. Puree this mixture in a blender for 2 minutes.

2. If desired, strain the mixture to remove lumps. Return the mixture to the bowl. Add the vinegar, garlic, and salt. Process the entire mixture in the blender again for another 2 minutes. Cover and refrigerate 1–24 hours. To serve, garnish with parsley sprigs. Serve the remaining diced vegetables in their separate bowls so each diner may add garnishes as desired.

10 servings
Serving size: 1 cup
Vegetable Exchange 3
Calories..............................75
Total Fat..........................0 g
    Calories from Fat.........0
Cholesterol ....0 mg
Sodium ....165 mg
Carbohydrate...............15 g
    Dietary Fiber.............2 g
Protein............................3 g

Spanish Tortilla

3 medium potatoes, peeled
   and cut into 1/2-inch cubes
5 tsp olive oil
1/2 cup diced green pepper
1/2 cup diced onion
2 Tbsp chopped parsley

1/2 cup chopped tomato
1 cup egg substitute
1/2 tsp pepper
1 tsp salt
Nonstick cooking spray

1. Preheat the oven to 425°F. Boil potatoes for 20 minutes or until tender. Place the potatoes in a large bowl and add 3 tsp olive oil. Gently mix the potatoes until they are well coated with the oil. Place the potatoes on a cookie sheet and bake for 25 minutes.

8 servings
Serving size: 1/8 recipe
Starch Exchange................1
Fat Exchange...................1/2
Calories 100
Total Fat.........................3 g
   Calories from Fat.......27
Cholesterol ....0 mg
Sodium......................312 mg
Carbohydrate...............13 g
   Dietary Fiber ....1 g
Protein ....5 g

2. Meanwhile, in a medium pan, heat 2 tsp olive oil and saute the green pepper, onion, parsley, and tomato. When the onion is translucent, remove the pan from the heat. Combine the egg substitute, onion mixture, and potatoes in a bowl. Add the pepper and salt and mix well.

3. Decrease the oven temperature to 375°F. Spray an 8-inch round cake pan with nonstick cooking spray; pour the mixture into the cake pan; and bake for an additional 20–25 minutes, or until the top begins to brown.

Ensalada Catalana

1 medium eggplant
3 medium green peppers
3 medium onions
3 medium tomatoes
2 7-oz cans artichoke hearts
6 tsp olive oil
2 cloves garlic, minced
1/4 cup chopped parsley
2 Tbsp capers in vinegar
1/8 tsp white pepper
1/4 tsp salt
2 lemons
1 hard-boiled egg

1. Preheat the oven to 300°F. Place the eggplant, green pepper, onion, and tomatoes in a covered dish and roast for 60 minutes. Allow the vegetables to cool to room temperature, then peel and remove all seeds. Slice the vegetables into strips and add the artichoke hearts. Set aside.

2. Heat 1 tsp of the olive oil in a small skillet and saute the garlic for 3–4 minutes. Add the parsley, capers, pepper, and salt. Squeeze the lemons and add the juice to the remaining oil. Mix this well with the garlic; then pour over the vegetables. Toss gently to coat and refrigerate before serving. Garnish with sliced egg.

18 servings
Serving size: 1/2 cup
Vegetable Exchange...........1
Fat Exchange...................1/2
Calories............................51
Total Fat ....2 g
   Calories from Fat 18
Cholesterol ....15 mg
Sodium.....................58 mg
Carbohydrate ....8 g
   Dietary Fiber ....1 g
Protein ....2 g

Dhal

8 oz chanadhal (yellow split peas)
1 tsp turmeric
1/2 tsp salt
2 green chilis, split lengthwise
1 Tbsp corn oil
1 tsp mustard seed
1 medium onion, finely sliced
1 clove garlic, finely sliced
1/2 tsp cayenne pepper

1. Wash the peas in cold, running water. When the water runs clear, set the peas aside to soak for 4 hours. Drain the peas and put in a saucepan with the turmeric, salt, and green chilis. Add enough water to cover by 1 inch and bring to a boil.

2. Partly cover the pan, reduce heat, and simmer for 1 hour, or until the water has been absorbed and the peas are tender, but not mushy. Add more water if necessary.

6 servings
Serving size: 1/6 recipe
Starch Exchange...............1
Vegetable Exchange..........1
Calories...........................123
Total Fat........................2 g
   Calories from Fat.......18
Cholesterol.................0 mg
Sodium......................151 mg
Carbohydrate...............19 g
   Dietary Fiber..............2 g
Protein...........................7 g

3. Meanwhile, heat the corn oil in a skillet. Add the mustard seed and cover the pan. Saute for 2 minutes. Uncover the pan, add the onion and garlic, and saute until golden. Stir in the cayenne pepper and cook for 30 seconds. Add the mixture to the peas, stir, and cook for 2 minutes. Serve hot.

Shami Kabob

1/2 cup chanadhal (dried split peas, yellow or green)
Enough water to cover
3 cups water
1 lb very lean ground beef
1 tsp cumin seed
1-inch piece cinnamon stick
6 whole cloves
1-inch piece fresh ginger root, peeled

8 cloves garlic
1–2 tsp chili powder
1/2 tsp salt
1/2 cup egg substitute
1 onion, chopped
1/3 cup chopped cilantro
3 green chilis, chopped

1. Soak the peas in water for 10 minutes, then drain. Put the 3 cups of water in a large skillet and boil the ground beef, peas, and next 7 ingredients for 45 minutes, or until all liquid evaporates. Allow the mixture to cool slightly. Add the egg substitute.

2. Using a blender or food processor, grind the meat mixture to a fine paste. Add the onion, cilantro, and chilis. Preheat the oven to 350°F. Line a cookie sheet with aluminum foil, or spray with nonstick cooking spray. Measure 1/4-cup portions onto the cookie sheet and shape into patties. Bake for 25–30 minutes or until set.

7 servings
Serving size: 2 patties
Starch Exchange................1
Lean Meat Exchange 2
Fat Exchange 1
Calories...........................232
Total Fat.........................12 g
   Calories from Fat 108
Cholesterol................44 mg
Sodium ....250 mg
Carbohydrate ....12 g
   Dietary Fiber ....1 g
Protein ....18 g

Naan

2 cups flour
1/2 pkg dry yeast (1 1/2 tsp)
1/4 tsp salt
1/2 cup water
Nonstick cooking spray

1. Combine all ingredients to form a dough. Let the dough rise until it doubles, about 1 hour. Punch the dough down and divide it into 10 parts. Roll each part into a thin circle. Brush one side with water.

2. Preheat the oven to 400°F. Spray a griddle with nonstick cooking spray. Put the circles on the hot griddle, watered side up. Cook until half done or lightly browned, about 3 minutes. Transfer to a nonstick cookie sheet. Bake for an additional 5–10 minutes.

10 servings
Serving size: 1 piece
Starch Exchange...............1
Calories 85
Total Fat.........................0 g
    Calories from Fat.........0
Cholesterol ....0 mg
Sodium......................59 mg
Carbohydrate ....17 g
    Dietary Fiber.............0 g
Protein ....3 g

Sadiq's Rice Pudding

1/2 cup white rice (basmati, if available)
3/4 cup water
2 cups skim milk
1 tsp vanilla
3 tsp sugar substitute
1/2 cup raisins
1 cup nondairy whipped topping
6 sprigs mint

1. Soak the rice in 3/4 cup water for 1 hour, then cook rice in the same water until thick. Add the milk. Cook slowly, stirring occasionally, until thickened, but stop cooking before all of the liquid is absorbed.

2. Allow the rice to cool, then add the vanilla, sugar substitute, and raisins. Fold in the whipped topping. Spoon into 6 serving dishes. Garnish with a sprig of mint and serve.

6 servings
Serving size: 1/6 recipe
Starch Exchange 2
Fat Exchange 1
Calories 170
Total Fat ....4 g
    Calories from Fat 36
Cholesterol ....2 mg
Sodium ....48 mg
Carbohydrate ....30 g
    Dietary Fiber ....1 g
Protein ....4 g

Mushrooms Italiano

1 lb medium mushrooms, cleaned
2 Tbsp margarine
1 medium onion, finely chopped
1/4 cup finely chopped green pepper
1 small clove garlic, minced
1 1/2 oz Canadian bacon, finely chopped
1/3 cup low-fat, low-sodium chicken broth
12 wheat crackers, finely crushed
1/2 tsp seasoning salt
Pepper to taste
1/4 tsp oregano
3 Tbsp Parmesan cheese

1. Remove the mushroom stems, set the caps aside, and chop the stems. Melt the margarine in a skillet and saute the stems, onion, green pepper, garlic, and bacon until tender, not brown. Remove from heat.

6 servings
Serving size: 1/6 of recipe
Vegetable Exchange...........1
Fat Exchange................1 1/2
Calories 109
Total Fat ....7 g
    Calories from Fat......63
Carbohydrate.................7 g
Protein ....5 g

2. Preheat the oven to 325°F. Mix the remaining ingredients in a separate bowl and add to the sauted vegetables. Pack the mixture lightly into the mushroom caps.

3. Place the mushrooms in a baking pan with a small amount of water in the bottom (too much water will make the mushrooms soggy). Bake for 20 minutes.

Eggplant Parmesan

1 1/2 lb eggplant
Nonstick cooking spray
1/4 cup water
1 pt part-skim ricotta cheese
1 15-oz can (1 2/3 cups) tomato sauce
1 garlic clove, crushed
1 Tbsp basil
1/2 tsp oregano
1/2 cup Italian seasoned bread crumbs
2 Tbsp Parmesan cheese, grated

1. Peel the eggplant and cut into 1/4-inch slices. Spray a large skillet with nonstick cooking spray. Layer the eggplant slices in the skillet, add the water, and cover. Simmer until tender, adding more water if necessary.

2. Preheat the oven to 350°F. Drain the eggplant on paper towels. Place half of the slices in a 12 x 7 1/2 x 2-inch baking dish. Spread half of the ricotta cheese over the eggplant. Combine the tomato sauce, garlic, basil, and oregano. Pour half of sauce mixture over the ricotta.

3. Combine the bread crumbs and Parmesan cheese. Sprinkle half over the top of the sauce mixture. Repeat the eggplant, cheese, sauce, and bread crumb layers. Bake for 30 minutes or until the sauce is bubbly.

8 servings
Serving size: 1/8 recipe
Vegetable Exchange..........2
Medium-Fat Meat
    Exchange........................1
Calories........................141
Total Fat........................5 g
    Calories from Fat......45
Carbohydrate..............12 g
Protein............................9 g

Italy

Mediterranean Pita Pizza

2 Tbsp olive oil
2 1/2 cups peeled and diced eggplant
1 cup sliced zucchini or yellow squash
1 cup sliced fresh mushrooms
1/2 cup ripe olives, pitted and sliced
1/4 cup chopped green pepper
1/4 cup chopped onion
1 garlic clove, crushed
2 Tbsp water
1 8-oz can pizza sauce
1/8 tsp cayenne pepper
6 pita breads
1 1/2 cups shredded mozzarella cheese

1. Heat the oil in a large skillet and saute the eggplant, zucchini, mushrooms, olives, green pepper, onion, and garlic for 5–6 minutes. Stir in the water, pizza sauce, and cayenne pepper. Simmer 5 minutes.

2. Preheat the oven to broil. Separate each pita bread into two rounds. Toast the rounds of pita bread for 1–2 minutes under the broiler.

12 servings
Serving size: 1 pizza
Starch Exchange 2
Vegetable Exchange...........1
Medium-Fat Meat
    Exchange 1
Calories 227
Total Fat ....7 g
    Calories from Fat......63
Carbohydrate ....33 g
Protein............................8 g

3. Spoon 1/2 cup of the vegetable mixture onto each bread. Top with shredded cheese. Broil until cheese melts, about 1 minute.

Seafood Marinara

2 Tbsp olive oil
1 medium onion, chopped
1 medium green pepper,
    chopped
1 carrot, peeled and finely
    chopped
1 cup sliced mushrooms
2 cloves garlic, crushed
1/3 cup canned baby peas,
    drained
1/2 cup red wine

1 6-oz can tomato paste
1 1/2 tsp basil
1 tsp oregano
1/4 tsp pepper
3/4 cup water
1/2 lb fresh or frozen large
    shrimp, peeled and
    deveined
1/2 lb fresh or frozen scallops
1/4 cup grated Romano
    cheese (optional)

1. Heat the oil in a large skillet and sauté the onion for 1–2 minutes. Add the green pepper, carrot, mushrooms, and garlic; sauté until the vegetables are tender.

6 servings
Serving size: 1/6 recipe
Starch Exchange............1/2
Lean Meat Exchange 2
Calories 147
Total Fat.........................5 g
    Calories from Fat 45
Carbohydrate ....9 g
Protein...........................15 g

2. Add the peas, wine, tomato paste, basil, oregano, and pepper, stirring well. (The alcohol in the wine will evaporate, leaving only the flavor.) Thin the mixture by adding water slowly until it reaches the desired consistency. Bring to a boil, reduce heat, and simmer for 5 minutes.

3. Add the shrimp and scallops; cook 3–5 minutes or until shrimp are done. Serve with grated Romano cheese, if desired.

Rosemary Chicken

1/4 cup flour
1 tsp salt
1/4 tsp pepper
1 lb boneless, skinless chicken breast, cut into pieces
2 Tbsp vegetable oil
1/2 cup water
1/2 cup white wine
1/4 cup baby pearl onions or chopped onion
2 Tbsp fresh or 1 Tbsp dried rosemary

1. Combine the flour, salt, and pepper and place the mixture in a paper bag. Shake the chicken pieces in the bag to coat.

2. Heat the oil in a skillet and brown the chicken pieces. When evenly browned, add the water, wine, onion, and rosemary. (The alcohol in the wine will evaporate, leaving only the flavor.) Simmer for 30 minutes. Uncover and cook a few minutes more.

4 servings
Serving size: 3–4 oz
Starch Exchange............1/2
Medium-Fat Meat
    Exchange......................3
Calories...........................128
Total Fat......................13 g
    Calories from Fat.......117
Carbohydrate................8 g
Protein ....23 g

Italy

Chicken Sauce Picante

4 Tbsp low-fat margarine
2 lb chicken breast, 8 halves,
   skinned and deboned
1 tsp Cajun seasoning
1/4 cup flour
1 1/2 cups chopped onion
1 cup chopped bell pepper
1 cup chopped celery

2 cloves garlic, minced
1 14-oz can whole tomatoes
1 8-oz can tomato sauce
Hot pepper sauce to taste
4 Tbsp finely chopped parsley
4 cups plain, hot, cooked rice,
   unsalted

1. Heat 2 Tbsp margarine in a large skillet or Dutch oven. Sprinkle the chicken with Cajun seasoning and brown the chicken for 3–4 minutes per side. Set the chicken aside.

2. Brown the flour for 10 minutes in the skillet, stirring constantly. Add 2 Tbsp margarine and saute the onion, bell pepper, celery, and garlic until tender. Add the tomatoes, tomato sauce, and hot pepper sauce. Bring to a simmer and cook for 30 minutes, stirring frequently. Add water, if needed, to prevent sticking.

8 servings
Serving size: 1/2 chicken
*   breast with 1/2 cup rice*
Starch Exchange 2
Vegetable Exchange..........2
Very Lean Meat
*   Exchange......................3*
Calories 312
Total Fat ....4 g
*   Saturated Fat............1 g*
*   Calories from Fat 32*
Cholesterol ....69 mg
Sodium...................408 mg
Carbohydrate ....39 g
*   Dietary Fiber.............3 g*
*   Sugars ....5 g*
Protein ....30 g

3. Add the browned chicken. Simmer for an additional 45 minutes or until the chicken is tender. Sprinkle with parsley during the last few minutes. Serve over rice.

Shrimp Etouffee

1/2 cup flour
2 cups water
1/4 cup chopped green onion
1 1/2 cups finely chopped yellow onion
1 cup finely chopped bell pepper
1/2 cup finely chopped celery
1 1/4 lb large, unshelled shrimp, or 1 lb frozen, peeled shrimp
1 tsp Cajun seasoning
1/2 cup reduced-fat cream of mushroom soup (no water added)
3 Tbsp finely chopped parsley
2 cups plain, hot, cooked rice (unsalted)

1. Brown the flour for 10 minutes in a large nonstick skillet, stirring constantly. Add the water and cook for 30 minutes over medium-low heat. Add the onion, bell pepper, and celery and cook an additional 30 minutes.

2. Sprinkle the shrimp with Cajun seasoning and add the shrimp and soup to the skillet. Cook an additional 20 minutes over low heat. Sprinkle with parsley during the last few minutes. Serve over rice.

4 servings
Serving size: 1/4 recipe
Starch Exchange 3
Very Lean Meat
    Exchange 2
Calories 307
Total Fat ....2 g
    Saturated Fat...........0 g
    Calories from Fat........21
Cholesterol ....167 mg
Sodium ....593 mg
Carbohydrate ....47 g
    Dietary Fiber..............3 g
    Sugars ....6 g
Protein ....23 g

Lagniappe Bread Pudding

1 10-oz stale French baguette
1 qt skim milk
3/4 cup egg substitute
2 Tbsp vanilla
1 tsp almond extract
1/2 cup raisins

1 tsp cinnamon
3/4 cup sugar
Nonstick cooking spray
1/4 tsp cream of tartar
3 egg whites

1. Preheat the oven to 350°F. Soak the bread in the milk, leaving the crust on. Add the egg substitute, 1 Tbsp of the vanilla, the almond extract, raisins, cinnamon, and 1/2 cup of the sugar. Stir well.

2. Spray a thick-sided, preferably glass, 9 x 13-inch pan with nonstick cooking spray. Pour the mixture into the pan and bake 35–40 minutes. Meanwhile, beat the cream of tartar and the egg whites with an electric beater until the meringue is stiff but not dry, gradually adding the remaining 1 Tbsp vanilla and 1/4 cup sugar.

20 servings
Serving size: 1 square
Starch Exchange................1
Calories 95
Total Fat ....1 g
  Saturated Fat...........0 g
  Calories from Fat........5
Cholesterol....................1 mg
Sodium.......................113 mg
Carbohydrate................19 g
  Dietary Fiber..............0 g
  Sugars.......................12 g
Protein ....4 g

3. Carefully remove the pudding from the oven and spread the meringue over the top. Return the pudding to the oven and bake an additional 10 minutes, or until the meringue is slightly browned. The pudding should be firm when pierced with a fork. Allow to stand for 5 minutes before cutting into 20 squares.

Low-Fat Hummus Dip

1 16-oz can garbanzo beans (chickpeas)
1 tsp tahini
1 tsp extra-virgin olive oil
1 tsp chopped garlic
1 Tbsp water
1/4 tsp pepper
2 tsp fresh lemon juice
Cayenne pepper to taste
1/2 tsp cumin
1/8 tsp salt
2 hard-boiled eggs, yolks removed
2 Tbsp chopped black olives
1 sprig parsley

1. Drain and rinse the garbanzo beans. Try to remove as much of the loose outer covering of the beans during the rinsing process as possible. Discard these outer coverings.

2. Process all ingredients except the eggs, olives, and parsley in a blender or food processor until smooth. Place in a serving dish.

3. Remove the egg yolks and save for another recipe or discard. Chop the egg whites into small pieces, mix with the olives, and sprinkle over the dip. Garnish with parsley to serve.

4 servings
Serving size: 1/4 cup
Starch Exchange................1
Lean Meat Exchange........1
Fat Exchange..................1/2
Calories...........................512
Total Fat.........................5 g
   Saturated Fat.............1 g
   Calories from Fat......45
Cholesterol...............53 mg
Sodium....................208 mg
Carbohydrate..............20 g
   Dietary Fiber.............4 g
   Sugars.......................4 g
Protein............................8 g

Mediterranean

Light Lentil Soup

2 Tbsp extra-virgin olive oil
1 large onion, sliced
3 cups brown lentils, rinsed
  well
1 cup chopped celery
1 tsp chopped garlic
7 cups water
1 cup chopped carrots
1 14-oz can low-fat, low-
  sodium chicken broth

1 1/2 tsp cumin
1/4 tsp coriander
2 tsp balsamic vinegar
Chopped jalapeno peppers to
  taste
1/2 tsp pepper
Juice of 1/2 lemon
1/4 tsp salt
4–5 whole black peppercorns
3/4 cup chopped cilantro

1. Heat the oil in a large stockpot and saute the onion for 10 minutes. Add the remaining ingredients except the cilantro. Stir well after each addition.

2. Bring the soup to a boil, cover, and reduce heat. Simmer for 1 hour or until most of the liquid has been reduced. (There will not be much liquid left.) Top with cilantro before serving.

8 servings
Serving size: 1 1/2 cups
Starch Exchange..............3
Very Lean Meat
      Exchange.......................2
Calories........................309
Total Fat.........................5 g
      Saturated Fat............1 g
      Calories from Fat.......42
Cholesterol..................0 mg
Sodium.....................133 mg
Carbohydrate..............49 g
      Dietary Fiber............24 g
      Sugars.......................8 g
Protein.........................22 g

Mediterranean Black Bean Salad

4 cups Swiss chard or fresh
   spinach leaves, torn into
   large pieces
3 cups cooked basmati rice,
   cooled
1/4 cup water
1 16-oz can black beans,
   drained and rinsed
1 tsp cumin
1/2 tsp coriander
Fresh ground pepper to taste
Cayenne pepper to taste

1 1/2 cups diced tomatoes
4 oz feta cheese
1 Tbsp pine nuts
2 small cucumbers, peeled
   and sliced
3 Kalamata or large black
   olives, cut in half
1 fresh lemon, cut into several
   wedges
2 tsp extra-virgin olive oil
3 Tbsp balsamic vinegar

1. Wash and blot dry the pieces
   of Swiss chard or spinach.
   Arrange them on a large platter
   and top with the rice. Heat the
   water, beans, cumin, coriander,
   and pepper in a medium
   saucepan for 5–7 minutes,
   stirring to prevent sticking.

2. Spoon the beans over the rice.
   Top the beans with the tomato
   and sprinkle with feta cheese
   and pine nuts. Insert the
   cucumber slices along the rim
   of the platter. Place the olives
   on top of some of the
   cucumber slices. Place the
   lemon wedges around the
   platter. Drizzle the oil and
   vinegar over the entire platter.
   Serve warm.

4 servings
Serving size: 1/4 recipe
Starch Exchange 4
Very Lean Meat
   Exchange 1
Fat Exchange 1
Calories 406
Total Fat ....11 g
   Saturated Fat...........5 g
   Calories from Fat......99
Cholesterol...............25 mg
Sodium ....533 mg
Carbohydrate ....62 g
   Dietary Fiber ....10 g
   Sugars.........................7 g
Protein ....17 g

Easy Eggplant and Sausage over Couscous

1 Tbsp extra-virgin olive oil
1 medium onion, peeled and diced
1/2 lb lightly smoked turkey sausage, thinly sliced
3 cloves garlic, peeled and chopped
1 yellow bell pepper, seeded and chopped into 1-inch pieces

1 1/2 cups fresh eggplant, cut into 1-inch pieces
1 14-oz can low-sodium tomatoes, undrained, diced
1 tsp cumin
Fresh ground pepper to taste
Cayenne pepper to taste
Chopped jalapeno peppers to taste
1/2 cup chopped parsley
2 cups cooked couscous

1. Heat the oil in a large skillet and saute the onion for 10 minutes. Add the sausage and garlic and continue sauteing for 10 more minutes, stirring constantly.

2. Add the remaining ingredients except the parsley and couscous. Stir well, cover, and reduce heat. Cook for an additional 15 minutes.

3. Just before serving, add the parsley and stir well. Serve on top of the couscous.

4 servings
Serving size: 1/4 recipe
Starch Exchange 2
Vegetable Exchange...........1
Medium-Fat Meat
      Exchange 1
Fat Exchange 1
Calories 279
Total Fat........................9 g
      Saturated Fat..........3 g
      Calories from Fat 81
Cholesterol ....30 mg
Sodium....................633 mg
Carbohydrate ....37 g
      Dietary Fiber.............4 g
      Sugars.......................10 g
Protein...........................14 g

Favorite Holiday Meals

Roast Turkey

1 8-lb turkey, fresh or frozen (not self-basting)
3 bunches fresh herb sprigs (can include thyme, rosemary, and sage)
1 onion, thinly sliced and separated into rings
1/2 tsp poultry seasoning
1/2 tsp salt
2 cups low-fat, low-sodium chicken broth

1. Preheat the oven to 325°F. Remove the giblets from the turkey, rinse the turkey with cold water, drain well, and pat dry. Loosen skin from breast and drumsticks with your fingers. Place the herb sprigs and onion rings underneath the loosened skin. Sprinkle the poultry seasoning and salt into the neck and body cavities.

2. Place the turkey, breast side up, on a rack in a roasting pan. Cover the turkey loosely with an aluminum foil tent, shiny side down. Roast for 2 1/2 hours, basting every 15–20 minutes with the chicken broth.

3. Remove the foil tent and bake for 30 more minutes or until a meat thermometer reads 185°F. Remove the turkey from the oven and let stand for 15–20 minutes before carving.

20 servings
Serving size: 3 oz
Lean Meat Exchange 3
Calories 148
Total Fat ....4 g
    Saturated Fat ....1 g
    Calories from Fat 39
Cholesterol ....64 mg
Sodium ....269 mg
Carbohydrate ....0 g
    Dietary Fiber..............0 g
    Sugars ....0 g
Protein ....26 g

Turkey Gravy

1 Tbsp low-calorie margarine
3 Tbsp flour
1 cup low-fat, low-sodium chicken broth
1 cup defatted turkey drippings (or another cup of low-fat, low-sodium chicken broth)
1/4 cup dry white wine (or white grape juice)
1/4 tsp salt
1/3 tsp pepper

1. Melt the margarine in a medium saucepan over medium heat. Stir in flour and cook for 1 minute, stirring constantly with a wire whisk.

2. Gradually add the remaining ingredients, stirring constantly. Bring to a boil, still stirring constantly. Reduce heat and simmer, uncovered, until the gravy is slightly thickened.

7 servings
Serving size: 1/3 cup
Fat Exchange...................1/2
Calories 31
Total Fat ....1 g
   Saturated Fat...........0 g
   Calories from Fat........12
Cholesterol ....0 mg
Sodium ....111 mg
Carbohydrate ....3 g
   Dietary Fiber.............0 g
   Sugars.......................0 g
Protein ....1 g

Oven-Made Apricot–Wild Rice Stuffing

1/2 cup wild rice
1/2 cup brown rice
2 1/2 tsp low-sodium chicken bouillon granules
1/4 tsp nutmeg
2–3 cups water, or as needed
3 cups sliced fresh mushrooms
3/4 cup chopped dried apricots
3/4 cup chopped celery
3/4 cup sliced green onion

1. Rinse the wild rice in a strainer under cold water for 1 minute. In a medium saucepan, combine the wild rice with the brown rice, bouillon, and nutmeg. Add 2 cups of water and bring to a boil. Reduce the heat, cover, and simmer gently for 45 minutes.

2. If most of the water has been absorbed, add more water. Then add the remaining ingredients. Cover and boil gently over medium-low heat for 10–20 more minutes, stirring frequently. (Vegetables should be just tender.)

3. Preheat the oven to 375°F. Again, if water has been absorbed, add another 1/3 cup water and transfer to a 2-qt covered casserole. Bake for 25–30 minutes.

16 servings
Serving size: 1/2 cup
Starch Exchange.................1
Calories.............................65
Total Fat.........................0 g
  Saturated Fat...........0 g
  Calories from Fat........4
Cholesterol ....0 mg
Sodium.........................9 mg
Carbohydrate...............14 g
  Dietary Fiber.............2 g
  Sugars ....3 g
Protein ....2 g

Party Pumpkin Pie

1/2 cup gingersnap crumbs
1/2 cup graham cracker crumbs
2 Tbsp margarine, melted
Nonstick cooking spray
1 egg
2 egg whites
1 16-oz can pumpkin
1/4 cup sugar
2 Tbsp molasses (blackstrap or mild)
1 tsp cinnamon
1/2 tsp nutmeg
12 oz evaporated skim milk

1. Preheat the oven to 350°F. Mix the gingersnap and graham cracker crumbs together with the margarine. Lightly coat a nonstick 10-inch pie pan with nonstick cooking spray. Press the crumb mixture into the bottom of the pie pan and bake for 7 minutes. Let the crust cool on a wire rack. Leave the oven on.

2. Whisk together the remaining ingredients until well blended. Pour the mixture into the partially baked pie crust. Bake for 40–50 minutes, or until the center of the pie does not jiggle when you put on an oven mitt and gently shake the pan.

10 servings
Serving size: 1 slice
Starch Exchange 1 1/2
Fat Exchange 1/2
Calories 136
Total Fat ....3 g
   Saturated Fat ....1 g
   Calories from Fat 25
Cholesterol ....26 mg
Sodium ....141 mg
Carbohydrate ....23 g
   Dietary Fiber ....1 g
   Sugars ....18 g
Protein ....5 g

Cornish Hens Baked in Cider

8 Cornish hens (1 1/2–2 lb each)
8 bay leaves
8 cloves garlic, sliced in half
1/3 cup olive oil
1 tsp thyme
1 tsp sage
1/2 tsp pepper
3 Tbsp cornstarch
1 cup apple cider
1 apple, washed, unpeeled, and sliced

1. Preheat the oven to 325°F. Remove the giblets from the hens, rinse the hens with cold water, drain well, and pat dry. Place a bay leaf and 2 garlic clove halves in the cavity of each bird. Brush each bird with olive oil.

2. Combine the thyme, sage, and pepper. Gently loosen the skin with your fingers and rub the seasonings mixture under the skin and inside the cavity of each bird. Close the cavities by securing with toothpicks. Place hens, breast side up, in roasting pans. Pour water into the pans to 1/8 inch deep. Bake the hens, uncovered, for 40–50 minutes.

16 servings
Serving size: 1/2 hen w/skin
Medium-Fat Meat Exchange.........................4
Monounsaturated Fat Exchange...........................1
Calories 354
Total Fat ....25 g
   Saturated Fat ....6 g
   Calories from Fat....228
Cholesterol..............150 mg
Sodium........................74 mg
Carbohydrate ....4 g
   Dietary Fiber.............0 g
   Sugars ....3 g
Protein..........................25 g

3. Combine the cornstarch and cider. Carefully add 3 Tbsp of the pan drippings to the mixture. Pour the cornstarch mixture over the hens and bake another 45 minutes. When the legs are loose and seem to fall away from the body, the hens are done. Garnish with apple slices and serve.

Crusty Rosemary-Garlic Potatoes

4 large baking potatoes, unpeeled, well scrubbed
Olive oil–flavored nonstick cooking spray
3 cloves garlic, minced
1 tsp paprika
1/2 tsp salt
Fresh ground pepper to taste
2–3 Tbsp chopped fresh rosemary (or 1 1/2 Tbsp dried)

1. Preheat the oven to 350°F. Cut each potato lengthwise into 8–10 wedges. Lightly coat the bottom of an 11 x 13-inch roasting pan with nonstick cooking spray.

2. Combine the potatoes and minced garlic and place them in the roasting pan. Spray the potatoes lightly with the nonstick cooking spray, stirring them to make sure all sides are thoroughly covered. Sprinkle with paprika, salt, and pepper.

8 servings
Serving size: 4–5 wedges
Starch Exchange 2
Calories 141
Total Fat.........................0 g
   Saturated Fat...........0 g
   Calories from Fat...........1
Cholesterol ....0 mg
Sodium.....................144 mg
Carbohydrate ....33 g
   Dietary Fiber ....3 g
   Sugars.........................3 g
Protein ....3 g

3. Bake, uncovered, for 30 minutes. Stir the potatoes and sprinkle with rosemary. Roast for 10 more minutes or until the potatoes are crispy and brown.

Holiday Snow Peas

Nonstick cooking spray
3/4 lb fresh snow peas (stems and strings removed) or 2 6-oz
  pkg frozen snow peas
1/4 cup chopped green onion
1 2-oz jar sliced pimentos, drained
1 Tbsp sherry or sherry vinegar

1. Spray a wok or nonstick skillet lightly with cooking spray. Stir-fry the snow peas and green onion over medium-high heat, stirring constantly, for 2 minutes.

2. Add the pimentos and sherry and stir-fry 1 more minute. The snow peas should be bright and crisp. Serve hot.

4 servings
Serving size: 1/4 recipe
Vegetable Exchange...........1
Calories.............................39
Total Fat..........................0 g
    Saturated Fat...........0 g
    Calories from Fat..........2
Cholesterol ....0 mg
Sodium..........................4 mg
Carbohydrate.................7 g
    Dietary Fiber..............2 g
    Sugars........................4 g
Protein ....3 g

Acorn Squash with Cranberry Sauce

1 12-oz pkg whole cranberries (do not use canned)
1 large thin-skinned orange, unpeeled, seeded, and chopped
1 large Red Delicious apple, unpeeled, cored, and chopped
1/2 cup water
1/2 tsp cinnamon
1/4 tsp ginger
3 Tbsp sugar
4 small acorn squash, about 1 1/2–2 lb each

1. In a small saucepan, combine the cranberries and orange and apple pieces. Add the water and bring to a boil. Reduce the heat and add the cinnamon and ginger; simmer until the mixture is soft. Remove from the heat and stir in the sugar.

2. Cut each squash in half and remove seeds. Place the squash, cut side down, in a steamer basket and steam for 15 minutes. The squash is done when a fork pierces the skin easily.

8 servings
Serving size: 1/2 squash
Starch Exchange...............1
Fruit Exchange...................1
Calories 136
Total Fat..........................0 g
   Saturated Fat...........0 g
   Calories from Fat.........3
Cholesterol ....0 mg
Sodium ....7 mg
Carbohydrate ....36 g
   Dietary Fiber.............9 g
   Sugars.......................21 g
Protein ....2 g

3. Stuff the cranberry mixture into the squash cavity. Steam the stuffed squash for 5 minutes or microwave for 1 minute.

Cranberry Cooler

4 cups low-calorie cranberry juice cocktail
2 6-oz cans unsweetened, frozen grapefruit juice concentrate
6 6-oz cans water
2 tsp coriander
4 tsp ground orange peel
20 round, thin orange slices

Combine all ingredients except orange slices and chill until ready to serve. Just before serving, float the orange slices in a punch bowl or on top of each glass.

12 servings
Serving size: 6 oz
Fruit Exchange....................1
Calories...........................60
Total Fat........................0 g
    Calories from Fat........0
Cholesterol ....0 mg
Sodium.......................2 mg
Carbohydrate..............15 g
    Dietary Fiber.............0 g
Protein.........................0 g

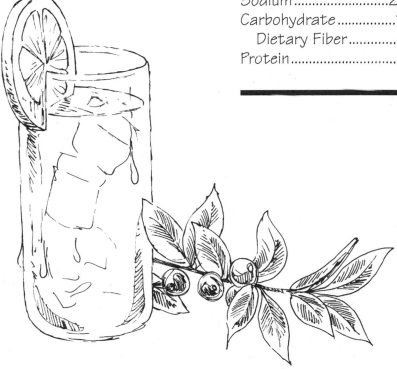

Beefy Vegetable Barley Soup

1 Tbsp vegetable oil
1 lb lean sirloin, well trimmed, cut into 1-inch cubes
2 small cloves garlic, minced
8 cups water
1 28-oz can tomato puree
1 beef bouillon cube
1/4 tsp pepper
1 bay leaf
1 1/2 cups sliced carrots
1 1/2 cups sliced celery (slice diagonally)
1/2 cup chopped onion
1/2 cup uncooked barley

1. Heat the oil in a large stockpot. Brown the beef and garlic. Drain off any excess fat, then add the water, tomato puree, bouillon cube, pepper, and bay leaf. Bring to a boil, then reduce the heat and add the carrots, celery, and onion.

2. Simmer the soup 1 1/2 hours, then add the barley and simmer another 20–25 minutes until the barley and meat are tender and the vegetables are soft. Remove the bay leaf before serving.

10 servings
Serving size: 1 1/4 cups
Starch Exchange................1
Vegetable Exchange...........1
Medium-Fat Meat
    Exchange 1
Calories 176
Total Fat.........................8 g
    Calories from Fat.......72
Cholesterol ....31 mg
Sodium ....450 mg
Carbohydrate...............20 g
    Dietary Fiber ....4 g
Protein...........................12 g

Valentine's Day

Vegetable Salad with Yogurt Dressing

3 sweet red onions, thinly sliced
3 or 4 red peppers, julienned
8–10 cherry tomatoes
10–12 radishes, cut into rosettes
1 cauliflower head, cut into flowerettes
1 head red cabbage, shredded
8 oz plain nonfat yogurt
1 Tbsp lemon juice
1/2 tsp cinnamon, cardamom, or ginger

Combine the vegetables and toss well to mix. Whip together the yogurt, lemon juice, and spice and drizzle over the salad. Serve chilled.

12 servings
Serving size: 1/12 recipe
Vegetable Exchange...........1
Calories 28
Total Fat..........................0 g
    Calories from Fat.........0
Cholesterol ....0 mg
Sodium ....13 mg
Carbohydrate................6 g
    Dietary Fiber ....1 g
Protein ....1 g

Crispy Chicken

1 cup cornflakes
1/4 tsp thyme
1/4 tsp pepper
1 lb skinless, boneless chicken breast
1 Tbsp margarine, melted

1. Preheat the oven to 400°F. Crush the cornflakes between two sheets of wax paper. Mix the crushed cornflakes with the thyme and pepper.

2. Rinse the chicken thoroughly and pat dry with paper towels. Place the chicken, breast side up, in a 13 x 9 x 2-inch baking pan. Brush the chicken with the melted margarine. Sprinkle the corn-flakes on top of the chicken breasts.

4 servings
Serving size: 3–4 oz
Starch Exchange.............1/2
Lean Meat Exchange.......3
Calories............................202
Total Fat ....7 g
   Calories from Fat......63
Cholesterol................73 mg
Sodium.......................173 mg
Carbohydrate.................6 g
   Dietary Fiber.............0 g
Protein............................26 g

3. Cover the baking pan with a lid or a large sheet of foil tucked under the sides of the pan. Bake for 30 minutes. Carefully remove foil, then bake, uncovered, for another 30 minutes.

Mother's Day

Polka-Dot Rice

1 tsp oil
2 1/2 cups water
1 cup brown rice
1/4 tsp basil
1/4 tsp sage
1 cup cooked green peas, hot

1. Add the oil to the water in a saucepan and bring to a rolling boil. Then add the brown rice, basil, and sage.

2. Lower the heat, cover the pan, and simmer for 45 minutes. Stir in the peas and serve.

8 servings
Serving size: 1/2 cup
Starch Exchange.................1
Vegetable Exchange...........1
Calories...........................105
Total Fat ....1 g
   Calories from Fat.........9
Cholesterol ....0 mg
Sodium.......................20 mg
Carbohydrate ....21 g
   Dietary Fiber..............0 g
Protein...........................3 g

Banana-Nut Gelatin Salad

1 3-oz pkg artificially sweetened strawberry gelatin
1 cup very hot water
1 cup cold water
1/2 cup unsweetened applesauce
1 banana, sliced
8–10 walnuts, chopped

1. Dissolve the gelatin in hot water. Add the cold water and stir. Chill the gelatin in the refrigerator until it begins to firm up (about 1 hour).

2. Stir in the applesauce, banana, and walnuts. Spoon gelatin into 4 individual dessert dishes. Chill before serving.

4 servings
Serving size: 1/2 cup
Fruit Exchange....................1
Fat Exchange 1
Calories 94
Total Fat..........................5 g
   Calories from Fat 45
Cholesterol ....0 mg
Sodium..........................3 mg
Carbohydrate...............13 g
   Dietary Fiber..............0 g
Protein ....2 g

Angel Food Cake with Fruit

1 cup strawberries, sliced
1 cup mandarin oranges, canned in their juice, drained
1/2 cup nonfat, artificially sweetened yogurt, any flavor
1/3 angel food cake

1. Combine the strawberries, oranges, and yogurt. Stir well. Slice the angel food cake into 4 pieces, using a gentle sawing motion with a bread knife.

2. Top each piece of cake with 1/4 of the fruit topping and serve.

4 servings
Serving size: 1 slice
Starch Exchange.........1 1/2
Fruit Exchange....................1
Calories.............................176
Total Fat ....1 g
   Calories from Fat.........9
Cholesterol....................1 mg
Sodium ....293 mg
Carbohydrate ....46 g
   Dietary Fiber..............0 g
Protein ....5 g

Oven-Fried Chicken

1 Tbsp canola oil
1/4 cup plus 2 Tbsp flour
1/2 tsp poultry seasoning
1/2 tsp seasoned salt
1/2 tsp pepper
1 1/2 lb boneless, skinless chicken breast

1. Preheat the oven to 400°F. Coat the bottom of a 13 x 9 x 2-inch baking pan with oil.

2. Combine the flour and seasonings in a paper bag. Dredge the chicken well in this mixture. Place the chicken in the pan and bake for 1 hour, turning once.

8 servings
Serving size: 3 oz
Starch Exchange.................1
Lean Meat Exchange........3
Calories 230
Total Fat..........................9 g
    Calories from Fat........81
Cholesterol ....80 mg
Sodium ....262 mg
Carbohydrate ....11 g
    Dietary Fiber..............0 g
Protein............................25 g

Father's Day

Bean Salad

1 16-oz can green beans
1 16-oz can kidney beans
1 16-oz can garbanzo beans
1 16-oz can wax beans
1 16-oz can black-eyed peas
1 16-oz can whole kernel white corn
1/2 tsp dry mustard
1/2 cup sugar substitute
1/2 tsp salt-free seasoning
1/4 cup salad oil
1 cup apple cider vinegar
1 medium onion, chopped

1. Drain and rinse all the canned vegetables and combine in a large bowl.

2. Mix the mustard, sugar substitute, and seasoning in a small bowl; add the oil, vinegar, and onion. Mix well.

3. Pour the dressing over the vegetables and chill before serving.

16 servings
Serving size: 3/4 cup
Starch Exchange................1
Vegetable Exchange...........1
Fat Exchange...................1/2
Calories............................132
Total Fat.........................4 g
  Calories from Fat......36
Cholesterol ....0 mg
Sodium ....332 mg
Carbohydrate ....21 g
  Dietary Fiber.............5 g
Protein ....5 g

Potato Salad

1 1/2 lb new potatoes, white or red
4 hard-boiled eggs, peeled
1/4 cup low-calorie mayonnaise
2 Tbsp skim milk
1/4 tsp salt
1 tsp prepared mustard
2 Tbsp finely chopped onion

1. Boil the potatoes with the skins on until done. Peel the potatoes while they are still warm, and cut into small pieces.

2. Cut one egg in half, remove the yolk, and place it in a large mixing bowl. Mash the egg yolk with a fork. Add the mayonnaise, milk, salt, and mustard. Mix well.

3. Chop the remaining egg white and 3 remaining eggs. Combine all ingredients and mix well. Chill thoroughly before serving.

8 servings
Serving size: 1/2 cup
Starch Exchange................1
Vegetable Exchange...........1
Fat Exchange 1
Calories...........................140
Total Fat ....5 g
    Calories from Fat 45
Cholesterol ....107 mg
Sodium......................152 mg
Carbohydrate...............18 g
    Dietary Fiber ....1 g
Protein ....5 g

Father's Day

Fruit Crisp

Nonstick cooking spray
3 cups sliced apples
1 16-oz can sliced peaches, packed in juice
1/2 cup rolled oats
1/2 cup whole-wheat flour
3/4 tsp cinnamon
3/4 tsp nutmeg
3/4 tsp cornstarch
2 Tbsp low-calorie margarine, melted

1. Preheat the oven to 375°F. Spray a 9 x 9-inch baking pan lightly with nonstick cooking spray. Put the apples and peaches in the pan, along with the peach juice.

2. In a separate bowl, combine the remaining ingredients. Stir half of this mixture into the fruit. Sprinkle the remainder of the mixture on top of the fruit and bake for 30 minutes.

6 servings
Serving size: 3/4 cup
Starch Exchange................1
Fruit Exchange...................1
Fat Exchange..................1/2
Calories..........................153
Total Fat.........................3 g
   Calories from Fat.......27
Cholesterol ....0 mg
Sodium......................48 mg
Carbohydrate..............31 g
   Dietary Fiber.............6 g
Protein ....3 g

Deb's Barbecued Chicken

1 1/2 lb boneless, skinless chicken breast
1 recipe Mild Barbecue Sauce (see p. 137)

1. Pour half of the barbecue sauce over the chicken and allow it to marinate 2–24 hours in the refrigerator.

2. Remove the chicken from the marinade, discard the marinade, and grill the chicken for 20–25 minutes, turning once and basting with fresh barbecue sauce.

6 servings
Serving size: 4 oz
   chicken with 2 Tbsp
   sauce
Lean Meat Exchange 4
Calories 199
Total Fat ....4 g
   Calories from Fat 36
Cholesterol ....96 mg
Sodium ....269 mg
Carbohydrate ....3 g
   Dietary Fiber ....0 g
Protein ....35 g

Fourth of July

Mild Barbecue Sauce

1/2 cup plus 1 tsp vinegar
1/4 cup water
2 8-oz cans tomato sauce
3 drops hot pepper sauce
1/2 tsp garlic powder
1/8 tsp cinnamon
1/8 tsp dry mustard
1/8 tsp allspice
1/8 tsp celery seed
1 tsp onion powder
1/4 tsp pepper
1 tsp paprika
1 bay leaf
12 tsp sugar substitute

1. In a small saucepan, combine all the ingredients except the sugar substitute. Cover and simmer 30 minutes. Cool and add the sugar substitute.

2. Place the barbecue sauce in a covered container and refrigerate overnight to allow the flavor to develop.

14 servings
Serving size: 2 Tbsp
Free Food
Calories.............................12
Total Fat.........................0 g
    Calories from Fat.........0
Cholesterol ....0 mg
Sodium ....185 mg
Carbohydrate ....3 g
    Dietary Fiber.............0 g
Protein.............................0 g

Grilled Vegetable Kabobs

2 medium zucchini, cut in 1-inch slices
3 boiling onions, cut in half
12 cherry tomatoes
12 mushrooms
1/2 cup low-calorie Italian dressing
3 Tbsp lemon juice

1. Place the vegetables in a medium bowl. Combine the dressing and the lemon juice and pour over the vegetables. Cover the bowl and allow the vegetables to marinate in the refrigerator for 3–24 hours.

2. Thread the zucchini and onions equally on 6 skewers. Grill the kabobs 6 inches from medium-hot coals for about 10 minutes, until the vegetables are crisp outside and tender inside. Wear oven-proof gloves and turn the kabobs frequently while grilling.

6 servings
Serving size: 1 kabob
Vegetable Exchange..........2
Calories...........................60
Total Fat ....1 g
   Calories from Fat.........9
Cholesterol ....0 mg
Sodium ....164 mg
Carbohydrate ....12 g
   Dietary Fiber ....2 g
Protein ....2 g

3. Remove the kabobs from the grill. Carefully thread the mushrooms and tomatoes onto the skewers. Return the skewers to the grill for another 5–10 minutes, until the mushrooms and tomatoes are tender. Continue to turn the skewers frequently while grilling.

Almond-Flavored Fruit Salad

1 cup part-skim ricotta cheese
4 tsp sugar substitute
1/2 tsp almond extract
2 Tbsp skim milk
4 cups watermelon balls
4 cups blueberries, rinsed and drained

1. Combine the cheese, sugar substitute, and almond extract in a small bowl and beat until well mixed. Gradually add the milk and continue beating until smooth.

2. Combine the watermelon and blueberries. Divide the fruit into 6 serving dishes. Pour 2 Tbsp of the cheese mixture over each dish.

6 servings
Serving size: 1/6 recipe
Fruit Exchange.....................1
Medium-Fat Meat
    Exchange 1
Calories...........................120
Total Fat ....4 g
    Calories from Fat......36
Cholesterol...............13 mg
Sodium ....41 mg
Carbohydrate ....17 g
    Dietary Fiber ....1 g
Protein............................6 g

3. This dish can also be served in a hollowed-out watermelon shell. Place the cheese mixture in a glass bowl inside the shell and arrange the fruit around the glass bowl. Let guests drizzle their own cheese on their fruit.

Fresh Tomato and Basil Salad

3/4 cup red wine vinegar
2 Tbsp olive oil
1/4 tsp garlic powder
1/8 tsp pepper
1/4 tsp salt
1/3 cup chopped fresh basil
4 tomatoes, cut into 4 wedges each

Whisk together all ingredients except the tomatoes. Pour the dressing over the tomatoes. Chill 4 hours before serving.

4 servings
Serving size: 1/4 recipe
Vegetable Exchange...........1
Fat Exchange 1
Calories 84
Total Fat ....7 g
   Calories from Fat......63
Cholesterol ....0 mg
Sodium ....146 mg
Carbohydrate ....5 g
Protein...........................0 g

Cinnamon Chicken Salad

1/4 cup low-calorie mayonnaise
1/4 cup nonfat plain yogurt
3/4 tsp cinnamon
1/8 tsp cloves
1/8 tsp pepper
1/4 tsp salt
1 1/2 lb boneless, skinless, cooked breast of chicken, diced
1/2 cup diced celery
2 Tbsp toasted slivered almonds
1 cup seedless grapes, halved

1. In a small bowl, whisk the mayonnaise, yogurt, cinnamon, cloves, pepper, and salt together.

2. Put the remaining ingredients in a large bowl and add the mayonnaise dressing. Toss well and refrigerate before serving.

6 servings
Serving size: 1 cup
Vegetable Exchange...........1
Lean Meat Exchange.......3
Calories.........................202
Total Fat........................8 g
    Calories from Fat.......72
Cholesterol ....64 mg
Sodium.....................247 mg
Carbohydrate ....5 g
Protein ....26 g

Minted Citrus Carrots

Juice of 1 medium orange
Juice of 1 medium lemon
1/4 cup chopped fresh mint
1/8 tsp pepper
3 large carrots, peeled and shredded

1. In a small bowl, whisk the juices, mint, and pepper together.

2. Toss with the shredded carrots and refrigerate. Serve cold.

4 servings
Serving size: 1/2 cup
Fruit Exchange....................1
Calories 52
Total Fat..........................0 g
  Calories from Fat.........0
Cholesterol ....0 mg
Sodium......................36 mg
Carbohydrate...............13 g
Protein.............................0 g

Fruit Trifle with Dressing

6 oranges, peeled, halved lengthwise, and sliced crosswise
3 bananas, sliced (dip in orange juice to prevent browning)
3 cups blueberries, fresh or frozen
2 1/4 cups seedless green grapes
2 1/2 cups halved strawberries, fresh or frozen
1 pkg artificially sweetened vanilla instant pudding
1 3/4 cups skim milk
3/4 cup plain nonfat yogurt
3 tsp orange zest (grated peel)

1. In a large bowl or trifle dish, layer the fruit in whatever order you wish. If you use frozen fruit, be sure to drain it well, or wipe it on a paper towel.

2. In a small bowl, combine the dry pudding mix and milk. Beat with a rotary beater 1–2 minutes until thickened.

3. Fold in the yogurt and add the orange zest. Spoon 1 Tbsp dressing over each fruit serving.

20 servings
Serving size: 1/2 cup
Fruit Exchange.....................1
Calories 76
Cholesterol....................1 mg
Sodium ....31 mg
Carbohydrate...............18 g
Protein ....1 g

Batter-Up Baked Chicken

1 cup plain nonfat yogurt
3 Tbsp sharp mustard
2 Tbsp purchased spicy herb mixture
Cayenne or fresh ground pepper to taste
1 large clove garlic, grated or minced
2 lb boneless, skinless chicken breast
2 cups crushed cornflakes
Nonstick cooking spray

1. Mix together the yogurt, mustard, herbs, pepper, and garlic. Dip each chicken breast in the yogurt-mustard mixture. Place the chicken pieces in a large baking dish. Pour any remaining mixture over them, and refrigerate, covered, at least 2 hours or overnight.

2. Preheat the oven to 375°F and coat both sides of each chicken piece evenly with the cornflakes. Lightly coat 2 heavy-bottom cookie sheets or 2 large oblong casserole dishes with nonstick cooking spray. Lay the chicken, rounded side up, on the baking sheets or casserole dishes.

3. Bake, uncovered, for 60–70 minutes or until the chicken is golden brown and juices run clear when the chicken is pierced with a fork. (If the chicken seems to be browning too quickly, lower the oven temperature to 350°F or cover chicken with a sheet of foil.) Serve hot or cold.

8 servings
Serving size: 4 oz
Starch Exchange 1 1/2
Very Lean Meat
     Exchange........................4
Calories 259
Total Fat........................4 g
    Saturated Fat............1 g
    Calories from Fat 32
Cholesterol................73 mg
Sodium....................365 mg
Carbohydrate..............24 g
    Dietary Fiber ....1 g
    Sugars ....4 g
Protein............................31 g

Winners' Coleslaw

4 cups raw cabbage, shredded into 1/4- to 1/2-inch pieces
1 medium apple, washed, unpeeled, and shredded
4 medium carrots, peeled and shredded
1 cup low-fat sour cream
2 Tbsp skim milk
1/2 cup fat-free mayonnaise
1 Tbsp white vinegar
1 tsp sugar

1. Mix the shredded cabbage, apple, and carrot together in a large bowl.

2. Combine the remaining ingredients in a separate bowl. Add the dressing to the slaw and mix well.

3. Cover the slaw and chill at least 1 hour or overnight. Keep chilled in a cooler until ready to serve. Toss lightly before serving.

8 servings
Serving size: 1/2 cup
Starch Exchange............1/2
Vegetable Exchange...........1
Saturated Fat
    Exchange 1/2
Calories...........................85
Total Fat.......................3 g
    Saturated Fat..........2 g
    Calories from Fat 23
Cholesterol................10 mg
Sodium.....................144 mg
Carbohydrate...............14 g
    Dietary Fiber.............3 g
    Sugars......................10 g
Protein ....2 g

50-Yard-Line Blueberry Cheese Pie

8 oz nonfat cream cheese
1/4 cup egg substitute
1 Tbsp plus 2 tsp sugar
1 6-oz store-bought reduced-fat graham cracker pie crust
2 cups fresh or unsweetened frozen blueberries, defrosted
1 Tbsp cornstarch
1/2 cup water

1. Preheat the oven to 325°F. Process the cream cheese, egg substitute, and 1 Tbsp sugar in a blender or food processor until smooth. Spread the cheese mixture evenly over the graham cracker crust. Bake for 20 minutes or until the cheese is firm. Cool and refrigerate.

2. Mix the cornstarch and water and heat on high in the microwave for 1 minute. Add this mixture and 2 tsp sugar to the berries and stir well. Cover and refrigerate for at least 4 hours or overnight.

6 servings
Serving size: 1 slice
Starch Exchange.........1 1/2
Fruit Exchange....................1
Lean Meat Exchange 1
Calories...........................232
Total Fat ....4 g
    Saturated Fat ....1 g
    Calories from Fat......38
Cholesterol ....6 mg
Sodium....................399 mg
Carbohydrate ....36 g
    Dietary Fiber ....1 g
    Sugars ....20 g
Protein...........................11 g

3. Just before serving, spread the blueberry mixture over the cheese layer. (Adding the blueberries earlier makes the crust soggy.)

Classics Served
with Verve

Basic Pizza Crust

1 cup warm water
  (105–115°F)
1 pkg active dry yeast
1/8 tsp sugar
2–2 1/2 cups white flour

1 cup whole-wheat flour
1 Tbsp olive oil
Nonstick cooking spray
2 Tbsp cornmeal

1. Pour the water into a large ceramic or glass bowl and sprinkle the yeast over the water. Add the sugar and stir to dissolve. Let the mixture stand in a warm place until it is bubbly, about 10 minutes. Add 2 cups white flour, the whole-wheat flour, and the olive oil. Stir until well mixed. Dough should be elastic, not sticky.

2. Spread 1/2 cup white flour on a smooth surface; place the dough on it and knead for 8–10 minutes. Lightly coat a large bowl with nonstick cooking spray. Place dough in the bowl and turn to coat with the spray. Cover the bowl with a clean towel and allow the dough to rise in a warm place until it has doubled in size, about 45–60 minutes.

3. Preheat the oven to 400°F. Divide the dough into two equal parts and shape each into a flat 12-inch round. Sprinkle 2 cookie sheets with cornmeal, place the crusts on the sheets, and prick them with a fork. Bake for 5–10 minutes. They are now ready to be topped with pizza filling.

12 servings
Serving size: 1/6 pizza
  crust
Starch Exchange 2
Calories 146
Total Fat ....2 g
  Saturated Fat...........0 g
  Calories from Fat........14
Cholesterol ....0 mg
Sodium ....1 mg
Carbohydrate...............28 g
  Dietary Fiber ....2 g
  Sugars...........................1 g
Protein ....4 g

Feta Cheese and Artichoke Heart Pizza

1 recipe Basic Pizza Crust (see p. 148)
1 large garlic clove, minced
2 Tbsp chopped fresh basil or 1 tsp dried basil
2 fresh plum tomatoes, thinly sliced
1/2 cup canned water-packed artichoke hearts, sliced
1/2 cup shredded, part-skim mozzarella cheese
2 oz feta cheese, crumbled
1 Tbsp Parmesan cheese

1. Preheat the oven to 400°F. Spread the garlic on each of the two pizza crusts and sprinkle with basil. Alternate tomato slices with artichoke hearts in a pinwheel pattern around the top of each pizza.

2. Sprinkle on the mozzarella, feta, and Parmesan cheeses. Bake the pizzas until the cheeses melt, about 5–10 minutes.

12 servings (2 pizzas)
Serving size: 1/6 pizza
Lean Meat Exchange 1
Starch Exchange 2
Calories 198
Total Fat ....5 g
    Saturated Fat ....2 g
    Calories from Fat.......42
Cholesterol ....11 mg
Sodium ....122 mg
Carbohydrate...............31 g
    Dietary Fiber ....2 g
    Sugars ....2 g
Protein...........................9 g

Pesto and Veggie Pizza

1 1/2–2 cups fresh basil leaves
3 cloves garlic
1/4 cup olive oil
1/4 cup Parmesan cheese
1 recipe Basic Pizza Crust (see p. 148)
1 1/2 cups broccoli florets, cooked tender-crisp
1 red pepper, julienned
1/2 cup sliced fresh mushrooms
1/2 cup shredded, part-skim mozzarella cheese

1. Preheat the oven to 400°F. Process the basil, garlic, olive oil, and Parmesan cheese in a blender or food processor until the mixture becomes a spreadable paste. Spread the pesto equally over the two pizza crusts, allowing a 1/2- to 1-inch empty border along the edges.

2. Place the broccoli and pepper on the crusts, alternating a broccoli floret and a pepper slice (florets facing outward), until all of the broccoli and peppers are used.

12 servings (2 pizzas)
Serving size: 1/6 pizza
Starch Exchange 2
Fat Exchange 1 1/2
Calories 233
Total Fat.........................9 g
   Saturated Fat...........2 g
   Calories from Fat 78
Cholesterol ....8 mg
Sodium......................96 mg
Carbohydrate...............31 g
   Dietary Fiber.............3 g
   Sugars ....2 g
Protein............................9 g

3. Lay the mushroom slices in the middle of each pizza; don't overlap the slices. Top each pizza with 1/2 of the mozzarella cheese. Bake pizzas until the cheese melts, about 5–10 minutes.

Spicy Chili

1 lb lean ground beef
2 medium green peppers, chopped
1 large onion, chopped
1 clove garlic, minced
1 jalapeno pepper, diced
1 16-oz can low-sodium tomatoes, liquid drained off
2 8-oz cans low-sodium tomato sauce
2 15-oz cans red kidney beans, rinsed and drained
1 1/2 Tbsp chili powder
1 tsp cumin
1/2 tsp pepper

1. Brown the beef in a large nonstick skillet until no longer pink, about 5 minutes. Add the green pepper, onion, garlic, and jalapeno pepper and continue to fry until the green pepper softens and the onion is translucent, about 5 more minutes.

2. Place the ground beef mixture into a 3-qt saucepan. Add the tomatoes, tomato sauce, kidney beans, seasonings, and enough additional water to cover the food. Simmer, covered, for 30 minutes.

4 servings
Serving size: 1/4 recipe
Starch Exchange 2
Vegetable Exchange..........2
Medium-Fat Meat
    Exchange........................3
Calories..........................460
Total Fat ....16 g
    Calories from Fat.....144
Cholesterol..................71 mg
Sodium ....342 mg
Carbohydrate ....46 g
    Dietary Fiber.............12 g
Protein ....35 g

Easy Meatballs in Spaghetti Sauce

1 lb lean ground beef
1/4 cup seasoned bread crumbs
1 egg, slightly beaten
1 Tbsp finely chopped onion
1 Tbsp chopped parsley
1 clove garlic, crushed
1/8 tsp pepper
1 26- to 30-oz jar low-sodium spaghetti sauce

1. Combine the ground beef, bread crumbs, egg, onion, parsley, garlic, and pepper, mixing lightly but thoroughly. Shape into twelve 1 1/2-inch meatballs.

2. Brown the meatballs in a large nonstick skillet for 6–8 minutes, turning occasionally. Add the spaghetti sauce and reduce heat to medium-low. Cover and cook for 10 more minutes, stirring occasionally.

This adapted recipe is courtesy of the Meat Board Test Kitchens and Beef Industry Council.

4 servings
Serving size: 3 meatballs
Starch Exchange 2
Vegetable Exchange...........1
Medium-Fat Meat
    Exchange........................3
Fat Exchange 2
Calories 484
Total Fat ....25 g
   Calories from Fat....225
Cholesterol...............124 mg
Sodium ....329 mg
Carbohydrate...............37 g
   Dietary Fiber.............0 g
Protein ....28 g

Italian Stir-Fry

1 lb lean ground beef
1 medium onion, chopped
1 medium green pepper, chopped
1 clove garlic, minced
1 large tomato, chopped
8 oz low-sodium tomato sauce
1/2 tsp basil
1/2 tsp oregano
4 cups cooked rice

1. Brown the ground beef in a large, nonstick skillet until the beef is no longer pink, about 5 minutes.

2. Add the onion, green pepper, and garlic and continue frying until the pepper softens and the onion is translucent; about 5 more minutes.

3. Add the tomato, tomato sauce, basil, and oregano. Simmer 10 minutes, uncovered. Serve over rice or pasta (not included in nutrient analysis).

4 servings
Serving size: 1/4 recipe
Starch Exchange 3
Vegetable Exchange..........2
Medium-Fat Meat
    Exchange.......................3
Calories 505
Total Fat ....16 g
    Calories from Fat.....144
Cholesterol ....74 mg
Sodium ....92 mg
Carbohydrate ....60 g
    Dietary Fiber ....4 g
Protein ....27 g

Mexican Stuffed Potato

1 large baking potato
4 oz lean ground beef
4 Tbsp nonfat sour cream
1 Tbsp mild salsa
2 Tbsp chopped green onion

1. Bake or microwave the potato so it is soft and ready to eat. Brown the ground beef in a large nonstick skillet until the beef is no longer pink, about 5 minutes.

2. Cut the potato in half lengthwise and scoop out the insides. Mix the beef with 2 Tbsp sour cream. Mash the inside of the potato with the beef–sour cream mixture.

3. Stuff the mixture back into the potato shell. Top with the remaining sour cream, salsa, and green onion.

1 serving
Serving size: 1 potato
Starch Exchange 3
Vegetable Exchange...........1
Medium-Fat Meat
      Exchange.......................3
Calories...........................487
Total Fat ....16 g
   Calories from Fat.....144
Cholesterol ....75 mg
Sodium....................200 mg
Carbohydrate ....56 g
   Dietary Fiber..............5 g
Protein ....29 g

Smothered Chicken

4 4-oz pieces boneless, skinless chicken
1/4 cup safflower oil
1 large onion, sliced
2 cloves garlic, minced
Fresh ground pepper to taste
1/2 tsp thyme
2 cups water
1 1/2 cups sliced carrots
1 1/2 cups green peas, fresh or frozen

1. Heat the oil in a deep sauce-pan or Dutch oven. Add the chicken and brown on both sides, about 3–4 minutes per side. Pour off the excess oil, then add the onion, garlic, pepper, and thyme.

2. Add the water, then cover the pot and bring to a boil. Lower the heat and simmer 2 1/2–3 hours. Add the carrots and peas. Cover the pot and return to a boil. Then lower the heat and simmer for another 20–30 minutes.

4 servings
Serving size: 1/4 recipe
Starch Exchange.................1
Medium-Fat Meat
    Exchange........................4
Calories 393
Total Fat.........................21 g
    Calories from Fat......181
Cholesterol ....101 mg
Sodium ....186 mg
Carbohydrate...............18 g
    Dietary Fiber.............5 g
Protein ....33 g

Spicy Greens

1 lb fresh spinach (or collard greens or kale)
1 Tbsp peanut oil
1/2 large onion, coarsely chopped
1 large tomato, chopped into small pieces
1/2 small lemon, sliced thin
Fresh ground pepper to taste
2 Tbsp curry powder, or to taste

1. Wash the spinach thoroughly. Cook in a saucepan over low heat about 5 minutes; do not add water. (There is usually enough water already clinging to the leaves to steam the greens.) Collard greens or kale may take 7–10 minutes.

2. Heat the oil in a skillet and saute the onion and tomato for 4–5 minutes. Add the cooked greens, lemon slices, and seasonings; stir constantly for a few minutes. Serve hot.

4 servings
Serving size: 1/2 cup
Vegetable Exchange...........1
Fat Exchange 1
Calories............................68
Total Fat..........................4 g
    Calories from Fat......36
Cholesterol ....0 mg
Sodium......................35 mg
Carbohydrate.................6 g
    Dietary Fiber ....2 g
Protein ....2 g

Hop'n John

2/3 cup dried black-eyed peas
2 1/2 cups water
1/4 cup leftover roast beef or turkey
1 small onion, finely chopped
Cayenne pepper to taste
1/4 tsp salt
Garlic powder to taste
2 cups cooked white rice

1. Rinse the black-eyed peas and drain. Put the peas in a saucepan, add enough water to cover, and bring to a boil. Cook over medium heat for 2–3 minutes; drain.

2. Cover with fresh water and add the meat and seasonings. Bring to a boil, then lower the heat and simmer for 2 hours, or until the peas are tender. If they dry out before they are done, add more water.

12 servings
Serving size: 1/3 cup
Starch Exchange.................1
Calories 81
Total Fat ....1 g
    Calories from Fat.........9
Cholesterol...................4 mg
Sodium ....52 mg
Carbohydrate...............14 g
    Dietary Fiber.............3 g
Protein ....4 g

3. Stir in the cooked rice and let the mixture simmer until all liquid is absorbed.

Candied Yams

6 medium yams, boiled in skin until tender (about 20–30 minutes)
1/3 cup raisins
1 Tbsp brown sugar
3 Tbsp sugar substitute
2 tsp cinnamon
1/2 tsp nutmeg
Ground cloves to taste
1/3 cup low-calorie margarine
1 cup cold water

1. Preheat the oven to 350°F. Cool yams, peel, and slice lengthwise. Place the yam slices in a covered baking dish. Sprinkle the raisins over the yams.

2. In a separate bowl, mix the brown sugar, sugar substitute, and spices; sprinkle over the yams. Dot with margarine and add water.

3. Cover the baking dish and bake for 30 minutes. Remove the cover, then bake another 15–20 minutes.

12 servings
Serving size: 1/4 cup
Starch Exchange.................1
Calories 81
Total Fat...................2 1/2 g
    Calories from Fat.......22
Cholesterol ....0 mg
Sodium......................63 mg
Carbohydrate...............14 g
    Dietary Fiber.............0 g
Protein ....1 g

Sweet Potato Pie

2 large sweet potatoes
2 egg whites, beaten
1 Tbsp sugar
1/4 cup raisins (optional)
1/2 tsp cinnamon
2 Tbsp low-calorie margarine
1 cup low-fat milk
1 9-inch ready-made pie crust

1. Wash the sweet potatoes and boil them in a covered saucepan until soft. Peel the potatoes and mash them in a medium bowl. (You should get about 1 1/2 cups of mashed potatoes.)

2. Preheat the oven to 450°F. Add all ingredients in the order given. Mix well and pour into the pie shell. Bake until lightly browned.

8 servings
Serving size: 1 slice
Starch Exchange 2
Fat Exchange 2
Calories.........................220
Total Fat.......................11 g
   Calories from Fat......99
Cholesterol ....3 mg
Sodium....................232 mg
Carbohydrate ....30 g
   Dietary Fiber..............0 g
Protein ....4 g

Salmon Loaf

Nonstick cooking spray
1 15 1/2-oz can salmon, undrained
2 eggs, beaten
2 cups soft bread cubes or 1/3 cup bread crumbs
2 Tbsp chopped parsley
1/8 tsp pepper
1 small onion, chopped
2 Tbsp lemon juice

1. Preheat the oven to 350°F. Spray an 8 x 4 x 2-inch loaf pan with nonstick cooking spray.

2. In a large bowl, flake the salmon, removing bones and skin. Add the remaining ingredients and mix well.

3. Press the mixture firmly into the loaf pan. Bake for 50–60 minutes until golden brown or until a toothpick inserted in the center comes out clean. Let stand at least 5 minutes before slicing.

6 servings
Serving size: 1 slice
Starch Exchange............1/2
Lean Meat Exchange 2
Calories.........................150
Total Fat.........................6 g
    Calories from Fat 54
Cholesterol..............103 mg
Sodium ....404 mg
Carbohydrate................8 g
    Dietary Fiber..............0 g
Protein ....16 g

Spicy Turkey Loaf

1 1/2 lb lean ground turkey
3/4 cup evaporated milk
1/4 cup finely chopped onion
1 cup bread crumbs
4 Tbsp chili sauce
1/2 tsp ginger
1/2 tsp garlic powder
1/4 cup chopped parsley

1. Preheat the oven to 350°F. Combine all ingredients and mix well. Press the mixture firmly into an ungreased 8 x 4 x 2-inch loaf pan.

2. Bake 45 minutes or until a toothpick inserted in the center comes out clean. Let stand at least 5 minutes before slicing.

8 servings
Serving size: 1 slice
Starch Exchange...............1
Lean Meat Exchange.......3
Calories 236
Total Fat ....19 g
   Calories from Fat.......171
Cholesterol ....72 mg
Sodium.....................278 mg
Carbohydrate...............14 g
   Dietary Fiber..............0 g
Protein...........................22 g

Prize-Winning Meat Loaf

1 1/2 lb lean ground beef
1 cup tomato juice
3/4 cup oats
1 egg, beaten
1/4 cup chopped onion
1/2 tsp salt
1/4 tsp pepper

1. Preheat the oven to 350°F. Combine all ingredients and mix well. Press the mixture firmly into an ungreased 8 x 4 x 2-inch loaf pan.

2. Bake for 1 hour, or until a toothpick inserted in the center comes out clean. Let stand at least 5 minutes before slicing.

8 servings
Serving size: 1 slice
Starch Exchange...............1
Medium-Fat Meat
     Exchange.....................3
Calories.....................292
Total Fat ....16 g
     Calories from Fat.....144
Cholesterol ....110 mg
Sodium ....402 mg
Carbohydrate...............10 g
     Dietary Fiber ....1 g
Protein............................24 g

Modern Meat Loaf

Lentil Loaf

1 cup lentils, rinsed
3 cups water
2 Tbsp margarine
7 1/2 oz grated cheddar cheese
1/4 cup minced onion
1/4 tsp thyme
1 egg, beaten
1/2 cup soft bread crumbs
1/2 cup coarsely grated carrots

1. Preheat the oven to 350°F. Spray an 8 x 4 x 2-inch loaf pan with nonstick cooking spray and set aside. Simmer the lentils in the water until tender (about 30 minutes).

2. Drain and mash lentils while they are hot. Combine the mashed lentils with the margarine, cheese, onion, and thyme. In another bowl, mix together the beaten egg, bread crumbs, and carrots. Combine with the lentil mixture.

5 servings
Serving size: 1 slice
Starch Exchange 2
Medium-Fat Meat
    Exchange........................2
Fat Exchange 2
Calories 359
Total Fat ....20 g
   Calories from Fat 180
Cholesterol..............100 mg
Sodium....................530 mg
Carbohydrate..............25 g
   Dietary Fiber ....4 g
Protein ....20 g

3. Press the mixture firmly into the loaf pan. Bake for 45 minutes, or until a toothpick inserted in the center comes out clean. Let stand at least 5 minutes before slicing.

Basic Polenta

4 cups water
1 tsp salt
1 cup yellow cornmeal
1 Tbsp grated fresh Parmesan cheese

1. Bring the water to a rolling boil in a heavy 2-qt sauce-pan. Reduce the heat so the water continues to simmer. Stir in the salt.

2. Pour the cornmeal into the water in a thin, steady stream. It's essential to stir the cornmeal and water constantly with a long-handled wooden spoon or a whisk as it cooks, about 40 minutes. This prevents the polenta from forming lumps.

6 servings
Serving size: 1/2 cup
Starch Exchange................1
Calories............................88
Total Fat ....1 g
    Saturated Fat...........0 g
    Calories from Fat........5
Cholesterol....................1 mg
Sodium.....................403 mg
Carbohydrate................18 g
    Dietary Fiber ....2 g
    Sugars ....0 g
Protein ....2 g

3. The polenta is done when it's smooth and thick and begins to pull away from the sides of the saucepan. Add the cheese and stir. Remove the saucepan from the heat and cover. The covered polenta will stay warm for about 20 minutes.

Polenta Italiano*

Nonstick cooking spray
12 oz low-fat Italian turkey
  sausage, sliced into 1-inch
  pieces
4 tsp red wine vinegar
1/3 cup low-fat, low-sodium
  chicken broth
2 medium green peppers, cut
  into strips
1 medium red onion

1 large clove garlic
1/2 tsp dried basil
1/2 tsp salt-free Italian
  seasoning
2 1/2 cups canned crushed
  tomatoes, juice included
2 Tbsp Parmesan cheese
1 recipe Basic Polenta (see p.
  164), prepared without salt
  or cheese

1. Lightly coat a large skillet with nonstick cooking spray and brown the sausage for 15–18 minutes. Add the vinegar and cook 1–2 minutes until the liquid evaporates. Add the next six ingredients. Continue cooking, stirring frequently, until the vegetables are tender, about 4–5 more minutes.

2. Stir in the tomatoes with their juice and the cheese. Bring to a boil, then reduce heat and simmer until the sauce thickens, stirring constantly, about 5–10 minutes. Serve over the Basic Polenta recipe.

* This recipe is high in sodium.

6 servings
Serving size: 3/4 cup sauce with 1/2 cup polenta
Starch Exchange 2
Vegetable Exchange...........1
Very Lean Meat
  Exchange 1
Fat Exchange...................1/2
Calories 248
Total Fat.........................6 g
  Saturated Fat...........3 g
  Calories from Fat......56
Cholesterol.................31 mg
Sodium ....923 mg
Carbohydrate...............35 g
  Dietary Fiber.............5 g
  Sugars.......................10 g
Protein...........................13 g

Polenta-Eggplant Casserole*

1 recipe Basic Polenta (see p. 164), prepared without salt or cheese
Nonstick cooking spray
2 medium eggplants, sliced into 1/2-inch circles
1 3-oz can sliced mushrooms, drained
1/4 tsp garlic
3 cups tomato sauce
3/4 cup shredded low-fat Mozzarella cheese
1/2 cup reduced-fat Parmesan cheese

1. Place the Basic Polenta in a 9-inch nonstick loaf pan and chill 4–24 hours, until the polenta is hard enough to slice. Then slice the polenta into 12 slices. Preheat the oven to 375°F. Spray a baking dish with nonstick cooking spray and arrange 6 polenta slices on the bottom of the dish.

2. Arrange the eggplant slices on top of the polenta. Top with the mushrooms. Add the garlic to the tomato sauce. Pour 2 cups of the tomato sauce over the eggplant and mushrooms.

6 servings	
Serving size: 1 cup	
Starch Exchange	2
Vegetable Exchange	2
Saturated Fat Exchange	1/2
Calories	224
Total Fat	4 g
Saturated Fat	2 g
Calories from Fat	39
Cholesterol	13 mg
Sodium	998 mg
Carbohydrate	36 g
Dietary Fiber	7 g
Sugars	12 g
Protein	12 g

3. Top with the remaining 6 polenta slices, then top with the remaining tomato sauce and the cheeses. Cover and bake until the eggplant is tender, about 45 minutes.

* This recipe is high in sodium.

Curried Hubbard Squash and Chicken

1 1/2 lb Hubbard squash
1 lb boneless, skinless
   chicken breast
3 pods cardamom
1/2 tsp cumin
2 tsp curry powder
1/4 tsp ginger
1/2 tsp pepper
1/2 tsp salt

1/8 tsp cayenne pepper
1 tsp turmeric
2 Tbsp olive oil
1 medium onion, finely
   chopped
2 cloves garlic
1 cup water
Juice of 1/2 lemon
Zest (grated peel) of 1 lemon

1. Peel the squash, slice off the ends, and discard. Cut the squash in half widthwise. Scoop out the seeds and discard. Slice the squash into strips about 1 inch wide and 4 inches long. Slice the chicken into strips about 1/2 inch wide and 2 inches long.

2. Combine the spices in a small bowl and set aside. Heat the oil in a large skillet and saute the onion for 3–5 minutes. Add the garlic and saute 1 minute longer. Add the spices and saute 3 more minutes.

3. Add the chicken strips and saute until the chicken is cooked through, about 5–7 minutes. Add the squash, water, lemon juice, and zest; simmer for an additional 10 minutes. Serve hot.

10 servings
Serving size: 3/4 cup
Vegetable Exchange...........1
Lean Meat Exchange 2
Calories 113
Total Fat ....5 g
   Calories from Fat.......45
Cholesterol ....38 mg
Sodium ....148 mg
Carbohydrate ....4 g
   Dietary Fiber ....3 g
Protein...........................14 g

Summer Squash Soup

1 1/2 lb zucchini
1 lb yellow summer squash
1 small onion, chopped
1 Tbsp olive oil
2 large cloves garlic
2 1/2 cups water
1 Tbsp dill
4 chicken bouillon cubes
2 Tbsp cornmeal
1/8 tsp pepper
Juice of 1/2 lemon

1. Wash the squash and cut the ends off. Puree the squash and the onion in a food processor or blender. Heat the oil in a large saucepan and saute the garlic for 2–3 minutes.

2. Add the water, dill, bouillon cubes, cornmeal, and pepper. Simmer, uncovered, for 5 minutes. Add the puree and simmer, uncovered, another 15–20 minutes. If soup is too thick, add water. Add the lemon juice and serve.

9 servings
Serving size: 1 cup
Vegetable Exchange...........1
Fat Exchange..................1/2
Calories 48
Total Fat ....2 g
    Calories from Fat 18
Cholesterol.....................0 g
Sodium...................388 mg
Carbohydrate.................7 g
    Dietary Fiber.............3 g
Protein ....2 g

Savory Squash

Apple-Scotch Squash

1 lb acorn squash
1 lb green apples, washed, unpeeled, and cut into slices
1 egg
1 cup skim milk
1 cup pancake mix
1 4-oz pkg artificially sweetened butterscotch pudding
1 cup water
Nonstick cooking spray

1. Preheat the oven to 300°F. Wash the squash, cut in half lengthwise, and bake 30 minutes. Peel the squash, discard seeds, and cut into 1/2 x 1/2-inch strips.

2. Mix the egg, milk, and pancake mix together until smooth. In a separate bowl, mix the pudding and water until smooth. Raise the oven temperature to 400°F. Spray a 4-qt casserole dish with nonstick cooking spray.

8 servings
Serving size: 1/8 recipe
Starch Exchange...............1
Fruit Exchange...................1
Calories...........................150
Total Fat ....1 g
   Calories from Fat.........9
Cholesterol ....27 mg
Sodium ....293 mg
Carbohydrate...............32 g
   Dietary Fiber ....5 g
Protein ....4 g

3. Layer the ingredients in the dish in this order: pancake mixture, apples, squash, and butterscotch mixture. Make 4 layers. Bake, covered, for 20–30 minutes. Remove the cover and continue baking for 10 minutes.

Chilled Yogurt Gazpacho Soup

4 cups plain nonfat yogurt
1/4 cup picante sauce
2 medium ripe tomatoes, quartered
3 green onions, including tops, quartered
1/8 tsp garlic powder
4 sprigs parsley or mint

1. Process all ingredients except the parsley in a blender or food processor until the soup reaches the desired consistency. For a chunkier effect, puree half the mixture, then combine it well with the unpureed half.

2. Chill before serving. For an elegant effect, pour the gazpacho into chilled stemware glasses and top with parsley or mint.

10 servings
Serving size: 1/2 cup
Skim Milk Exchange 1/2
Vegetable Exchange...........1
Calories 58
Total Fat.........................0 g
    Saturated Fat...........0 g
    Calories from Fat 1
Cholesterol..................2 mg
Sodium.....................166 mg
Carbohydrate ....9 g
    Dietary Fiber ....1 g
    Sugars ....8 g
Protein............................6 g

Spicy Lemon-Yogurt Chicken

6 oz low-fat lemon yogurt
Grated fresh ginger to taste
1/2 tsp paprika
1/4 tsp garlic powder
1/4 tsp coriander
2 whole chicken breasts, each split in half

1. Combine the yogurt, ginger, paprika, garlic powder, and coriander in a small bowl. Make three 1/2-inch deep slashes across each chicken breast to allow the marinade to penetrate the meat.

2. Place the chicken in a 2-qt baking dish and pour the yogurt marinade over it. Cover and refrigerate for 8–24 hours, stirring occasionally.

3. Preheat the oven to 375°F. Bake, covered, for 40–45 minutes, or until the chicken juices run clear. Serve hot.

4 servings
Serving size: 1/2 chicken breast
Starch Exchange............1/2
Very Lean Meat
    Exchange.......................4
Calories............................185
Total Fat..........................3 g
    Saturated Fat............1 g
    Calories from Fat........31
Cholesterol ....74 mg
Sodium......................88 mg
Carbohydrate ....8 g
    Dietary Fiber.............0 g
    Sugars........................8 g
Protein ....28 g

Salmon Steaks with Spinach-Yogurt Pesto

1 10-oz pkg frozen chopped spinach, thawed and well drained
1/2 cup fresh basil
1/3 cup Parmesan cheese
2 cloves garlic
1/2 tsp sugar
1/4 tsp nutmeg
1/4 tsp salt
1/4 tsp pepper
8 oz plain nonfat yogurt
2 lb fresh salmon, swordfish, or tuna steaks

1. Process all ingredients except the yogurt and fish in a blender or food processor until the mixture is just short of smooth. Add the yogurt and process the pesto until smooth.

2. Grill or broil the fish 4 inches from the heat source for approximately 10 minutes or until cooked. Spoon the pesto over the fish and serve.

12 servings
Serving size: 3 oz
Lean Meat Exchange.......3
Calories............................154
Total Fat ....7 g
　　Saturated Fat...........2 g
　　Calories from Fat......65
Cholesterol.................53 mg
Sodium ....159 mg
Carbohydrate ....3 g
　　Dietary Fiber ....1 g
　　Sugars ....2 g
Protein............................19 g

Date-Bran Muffins

Nonstick cooking spray
1 cup skim milk
2 large egg whites or 1/4 cup egg substitute
3 Tbsp vegetable oil
1 1/2 cups shredded bran cereal
3/4 cup chopped, pitted dates
1 cup flour
1/4 cup firmly packed brown sugar
2 1/2 tsp baking powder

1. Preheat the oven to 400°F. Spray a muffin tin with nonstick cooking spray or line with baking cups and set aside. In a large bowl, beat the milk, egg whites, and oil. Stir in the cereal and let stand 5 minutes. Mix in the dates.

2. In another bowl, combine the flour, brown sugar, and baking powder. Make a well in the center. Pour the date-bran mixture into the well and stir gently to combine.

3. Fill each muffin cup 2/3 full and bake until the muffins are golden brown and a toothpick inserted in the center comes out clean, about 16 minutes.

12 servings
Serving size: 1 muffin
Starch Exchange 2
Calories...........................153
Total Fat.........................4 g
   Calories from Fat......36
Cholesterol.....................0 g
Sodium.....................209 mg
Carbohydrate..............30 g
Protein.........................30 g

Blueberry Muffins

Nonstick cooking spray
1 3/4 cups plus 2 tsp flour
1 cup blueberries, picked over and rinsed
1 Tbsp baking powder
1/4 tsp nutmeg
1/4 tsp cinnamon
2 eggs
1/4 cup vegetable oil
3/4 cup orange juice
1 tsp lemon or orange zest (grated rind)

1. Preheat the oven to 400°F. Spray a muffin tin with nonstick cooking spray or line with baking cups and set aside. Lightly coat the blueberries with 2 tsp flour by shaking them together in a paper bag.

2. In a large bowl, stir together the remaining flour, baking powder, nutmeg, and cinnamon. In a small bowl, beat the eggs lightly. Add the oil, orange juice, and zest.

12 servings
Serving size: 1 muffin
Starch Exchange................1
Fat Exchange 1
Calories...........................140
Total Fat...........................6 g
    Calories from Fat 54
Cholesterol ....46 mg
Sodium......................95 mg
Carbohydrate...............19 g
Protein ....3 g

3. Add the liquid mixture to the dry ingredients and stir gently. Before the two mixtures are fully combined, fold in the blueberries. Fill each muffin cup 2/3 full. Bake for 20–25 minutes.

Marvelous Muffins

Double Corn Muffins

Nonstick cooking spray
1 cup flour
1 cup yellow cornmeal
1 Tbsp sugar
1 Tbsp baking powder
1/4 tsp salt
3 eggs (or 3/4 cup egg substitute)
1 cup low-fat cottage or ricotta cheese
1 8-oz can cream-style corn

1. Preheat the oven to 375°F. Spray a muffin tin with nonstick cooking spray or line with baking cups and set aside.

2. In a large bowl, stir together the flour, cornmeal, sugar, baking powder, and salt. In a small bowl, beat eggs and cheese until smooth. Stir in the corn.

3. Add the liquid mixture to the dry ingredients and stir just until blended. Fill each muffin cup 2/3 full. Bake for 25–30 minutes.

12 servings
Serving size: 1 muffin
Starch Exchange...............1
Lean Meat Exchange 1
Calories...........................139
Total Fat ....2 g
    Calories from Fat 18
Cholesterol...............70 mg
Sodium ....271 mg
Carbohydrate..............23 g
Protein.............................7 g

Very Berry Spread

4 Tbsp (1/2 stick) margarine, room temperature
2–2 1/2 Tbsp sugarless strawberry or other fruit spread

1. In a small bowl, beat the margarine until it is almost as creamy as sour cream. Beat in the fruit spread, 1 Tbsp at a time. The margarine will look curdled.

2. Put the spread into a serving bowl, cover, and refrigerate. The spread will keep at least 1 month. Let the spread soften at room temperature before serving (do not stir).

16 servings
Serving size: 1 tsp
Fat Exchange 1
Calories.............................37
Total Fat ....4 g
   Calories from Fat......36
Cholesterol ....0 mg
Sodium ....0 g
Carbohydrate ....0 g
Protein.............................0 g

Eating Green

Cuban Black Beans

2 1/2 cups dried black beans
Enough water to cover the beans
2 qt water
2 Tbsp olive oil
1 medium onion, chopped
1 green pepper, sliced
1 tsp oregano
1 bay leaf
1/4 tsp pepper
1/2 tsp ginger
1 tsp salt
1 tsp chili powder
2 tsp lime juice
2 tsp cumin

1. Cover the beans with cold water and soak them for 8–12 hours. Discard the water. Then combine all ingredients in a large stockpot. Bring the mixture to a boil over medium-high heat.

2. Once the mixture boils, reduce the heat and allow beans to simmer for 1 1/2–2 hours with cover slightly ajar. (The age of dried beans affects their cooking time. Older beans take longer; fresh beans cook faster.)

8 servings
Serving size: 1 cup
Starch Exchange........2 1/2
Lean Meat Exchange 1
Calories 233
Total Fat ....4 g
    Saturated Fat ....1 g
    Calories from Fat......38
Cholesterol ....0 mg
Sodium ....293 mg
Carbohydrate..............37 g
    Dietary Fiber............9 g
    Sugars........................6 g
Protein...........................13 g

Viva Vegetarian

Tofu-Spinach Lasagna

1 lb soft tofu
10-oz pkg frozen, chopped spinach, thawed and well drained
1 tsp oregano
1/2 tsp basil
2 cloves garlic, chopped fine, or 1/8 tsp garlic powder
4 cups low-calorie, meatless spaghetti sauce
1 cup water
8 oz whole-wheat lasagna noodles, cooked al dente
3 Tbsp Parmesan cheese

1. Preheat the oven to 350°F. Drain the tofu. Process in a blender or food processor for 30–60 seconds until it is creamy. Spoon the blended tofu into a bowl and add the spinach, oregano, basil, and garlic. Mix well.

2. In another bowl, combine the spaghetti sauce and water. Layer the lasagna ingredients in a 9 x 13-inch baking pan, starting with sauce, then pasta, then sauce, then tofu, then sauce. Repeat layers, ending with sauce. Sprinkle with Parmesan cheese.

3. Cover the pan with a lid or foil. Bake for 40 minutes, uncover, and bake an additional 15–20 minutes. Serve hot.

6 servings
Serving size: 1/6 recipe
Starch Exchange........2 1/2
Vegetable Exchange...........1
Lean Meat Exchange 1
Calories 275
Total Fat ....5 g
    Saturated Fat ....1 g
    Calories from Fat 46
Cholesterol...................2 mg
Sodium ....916 mg
Carbohydrate ....46 g
    Dietary Fiber ....11 g
    Sugars.......................14 g
Protein ....17 g

Marvelous Molasses Corn Bread

2 eggs, beaten
1 3/4 cups skim milk
3 Tbsp honey
3 Tbsp molasses
1/4 cup unsweetened applesauce
1 Tbsp baking powder
3 cups whole-grain cornmeal
1 cup whole-wheat flour
Nonstick cooking spray

1. Preheat the oven to 350°F. In a large bowl, mix the eggs, milk, honey, and molasses. Add the applesauce, baking powder, cornmeal, and flour. Don't overmix. The batter will be slightly lumpy.

2. Spray 2 loaf pans (or 18 muffin tins, or a combination of both) with nonstick cooking spray. Pour the batter into the pans and bake for 50–60 minutes. The corn bread is done when it pulls away slightly from the pan.

18 servings
Serving size: 1/18 recipe
Starch Exchange 1 1/2
Calories 134
Total Fat ....1 g
　　Saturated Fat...........0 g
　　Calories from Fat........13
Cholesterol ....24 mg
Sodium......................80 mg
Carbohydrate ....27 g
　　Dietary Fiber ....2 g
　　Sugars..........................7 g
Protein ....4 g

Chocolate Pudding

2 Tbsp cornstarch
2 Tbsp unsweetened cocoa powder
1/4 cup sugar
2 cups skim milk
1 tsp vanilla
1/4 tsp other extract, such as rum, almond, or orange, if
  desired

1. In a medium saucepan, combine the cornstarch, cocoa powder, and sugar. Mix well. Place over medium heat. Gradually add the milk, stirring to dissolve the cornstarch and cocoa into the milk.

2. Continue cooking over medium heat, stirring until the mixture comes to a boil. Continue boiling the mixture for 2–3 minutes, stirring constantly.

3. Remove from the heat and stir in the vanilla and extract, if desired. Spoon the pudding into 4 custard cups.

4 servings
Serving size: 1/4 recipe
Starch Exchange.........1 1/2
Calories 109
Total Fat ....1 g
    Saturated Fat...........0 g
    Calories from Fat.........5
Cholesterol....................2 mg
Sodium.......................64 mg
Carbohydrate...............23 g
    Dietary Fiber ....1 g
    Sugars ....17 g
Protein.............................5 g

Stuffed Pepper Salad

1 medium green pepper
1/4 cup alfalfa sprouts
1 medium tomato
1/4 medium cucumber, diced
1/4 yellow summer squash, diced
1 Tbsp fat-free Italian dressing

1. Slice the top off the pepper and set it aside. Clean out the membrane and seeds from inside the body of the pepper.

2. Combine the sprouts, tomato, cucumber, and squash. Add the dressing and toss lightly.

3. Pack the salad mixture into the prepared green pepper. Replace the pepper top and chill until ready to serve.

1 serving
Serving size: 1 pepper
Starch Exchange................1
Calories 71
Total Fat..........................0 g
    Saturated Fat...........0 g
    Calories from Fat.........6
Cholesterol ....0 mg
Sodium ....159 mg
Carbohydrate...............16 g
    Dietary Fiber ....4 g
    Sugars ....11 g
Protein...............................8 g

Red Onion Potato Salad

6 medium white or red potatoes (about 3 3/4 lb total),
   peeled, cooked, and sliced
1 cup sliced celery
1 cup thinly sliced red onion
1/3 cup chopped parsley
1/4 cup low-calorie Italian dressing
3 Tbsp wine vinegar
1/2 tsp salt
Dash cayenne pepper

1. In a large bowl, combine the still-hot cooked potatoes with the remaining ingredients. This will allow the potatoes to marinate in the dressing.

2. Refrigerate the mixture for several hours or overnight, so that it chills as it marinates. (Chilling the hot potatoes while they marinate brings out their full flavor.) Serve cold.

6 servings
Serving size: 1/6 recipe
Starch Exchange 3
Calories 221
Total Fat .... 1 g
   Saturated Fat .... 0 g
   Calories from Fat 12
Cholesterol .... 1 mg
Sodium .... 304 mg
Carbohydrate .... 49 g
   Dietary Fiber .... 5 g
   Sugars .... 7 g
Protein .... 5 g

Color Crunch Salad

3 cups canned black beans, drained and rinsed
2 medium tomatoes, chopped
2 medium red peppers, chopped
3 garlic cloves, minced
3 jalapeno peppers, chopped, or 1 small, green chili pepper, chopped
1 cup corn kernels, fresh or frozen
2 Tbsp chopped cilantro
1 Tbsp cumin
1/4 cup lime juice
1 Tbsp red wine vinegar
1 Tbsp olive oil

1. Combine all ingredients in a large bowl except the lime juice, vinegar, and oil. Cover and chill in the refrigerator for several hours.

2. In a small bowl, combine the lime juice, vinegar, and oil. Cover and refrigerate. Just before serving, add the dressing to the salad and toss well.

8 servings
Serving size: 1/8 recipe
Starch Exchange 1 1/2
Vegetable Exchange...........1
Calories 142
Total Fat ....2 g
   Saturated Fat...........0 g
   Calories from Fat........21
Cholesterol ....0 mg
Sodium ....122 mg
Carbohydrate...............25 g
   Dietary Fiber..............6 g
   Sugars ....6 g
Protein.............................7 g

Confetti Appleslaw

2 Tbsp frozen apple juice concentrate, defrosted
1 medium Red Delicious apple, washed, unpeeled, and diced
4 cups shredded green cabbage
2 small red onions, finely shredded
1 medium red or green pepper, thinly sliced
3 Tbsp raisins
1 Tbsp fat-free mayonnaise
1/2 cup plain low-fat yogurt
1/2 tsp dry mustard
Paprika to taste
Fresh ground pepper to taste

1. In a large bowl, stir together the apple juice concentrate and diced apple. Add the cabbage, onion, pepper, and raisins. Cover tightly and chill in the refrigerator for several hours.

2. In a small bowl, combine the mayonnaise, yogurt, mustard, paprika, and pepper. Mix well. Cover and chill in the refrigerator. Just before serving, add the dressing to the salad and toss well.

7 servings
Serving size: 3/4 cup
Starch Exchange...............1
Fruit Exchange...................1
Calories 77
Total Fat ....1 g
　　Saturated Fat...........0 g
　　Calories from Fat........6
Cholesterol....................1 mg
Sodium ....41 mg
Carbohydrate ....17 g
　　Dietary Fiber.............3 g
　　Sugars.......................13 g
Protein ....3 g

Celeriac and Potato Soup

2 lb celeriac
1 tsp vegetable oil
1/2 cup chopped onion
1 clove garlic, chopped
2 cups low-fat, low-sodium chicken broth
2 small baking potatoes, peeled and diced
2 cups skim milk
1/4 tsp salt
Fresh ground pepper to taste
2 Tbsp finely chopped parsley

1. Peel the skin and top knobs from the celeriac. Cut off the bottom, and trim the roots and leaves if they are still on. Dice the celeriac into 1/2-inch pieces. Heat the oil in a large saucepan and saute the onion and garlic until they are tender but not brown, about 5 minutes.

2. Add the chicken broth, celeriac, and potatoes. Simmer, covered, over low heat until tender, about 20 minutes. Remove the vegetables from the saucepan and puree them. Return the vegetables to the saucepan and add the milk.

3. Simmer the soup over low heat for 15 minutes. Do not allow the soup to come to a boil or the milk will curdle. Season with salt and pepper, sprinkle with parsley, and serve.

4 servings
Serving size: 1 cup
Starch Exchange 2
Calories 170
Total Fat ....3 g
 Saturated Fat ....1 g
 Calories from Fat.......24
Cholesterol ....3 mg
Sodium ....429 mg
Carbohydrate ....30 g
 Dietary Fiber ....5 g
 Sugars......................10 g
Protein ....9 g

Unbeatable Beets

1 Tbsp red wine vinegar
2 tsp prepared mustard
2 Tbsp lemon or lime juice
1 lb beets (leave some beet greens attached)
4 iceberg lettuce leaves

1. Combine the vinegar, mustard, and lemon juice and set aside. Boil the beets in 1 1/2 qt of water for 45 minutes. Leaving some greens attached keeps the beet color from bleeding into the cooking water.

2. Drain the beets, peel them, and remove the beet greens. Cut the beets into thin strips and combine them with the dressing. Serve the salad on lettuce leaves.

4 servings
Serving size: 1 cup
Vegetable Exchange..........2
Calories..............................56
Total Fat..........................0 g
    Saturated Fat...........0 g
    Calories from Fat 1
Cholesterol ....0 mg
Sodium ....117 mg
Carbohydrate ....12 g
    Dietary Fiber ....4 g
    Sugars ....8 g
Protein ....2 g

Dijon-Style Turnips

3 lb turnips
1 Tbsp olive oil
1/4 tsp salt
Fresh ground pepper to taste
1 cup low-fat, low-sodium chicken broth
2 tsp cornstarch
4 Tbsp Dijon mustard
1/4 cup chopped parsley

1. Peel the turnips. Heat the oil in a medium skillet and saute the turnips, salt, and pepper for 5–10 minutes until the turnips are softened. Add the broth, cover, and simmer until the turnips are tender, about 10 minutes.

2. Using a slotted spoon, transfer the turnips to a bowl and cover to keep warm. Reserve the vegetable juice in the skillet. In a small bowl, blend the cornstarch and mustard.

4 servings
Serving size: 1 cup
Vegetable Exchange..........2
Fat Exchange 1
Calories 84
Total Fat.........................5 g
   Saturated Fat............1 g
   Calories from Fat........41
Cholesterol ....0 mg
Sodium ....429 mg
Carbohydrate...............10 g
   Dietary Fiber.............3 g
   Sugars.......................6 g
Protein............................3 g

3. Add the mixture to the juice in the skillet and stir to blend. Simmer over low heat until the mixture is slightly thickened, about 1–2 minutes. Pour the sauce over the turnips and garnish with parsley.

Parsnip and Carrot Matchsticks

1 1/2 cups water
2 Tbsp low-calorie margarine
1 Tbsp brown sugar
1 Tbsp lemon juice
1/2 tsp salt
1 1/2 lb parsnips, julienned
1 1/2 lb carrots, julienned
1/3 cup chopped parsley
Fresh ground pepper to taste

1. Combine the water, margarine, brown sugar, lemon juice, and salt in a large saucepan, but don't turn on the heat. Stir to dissolve the sugar and salt. Add the parsnip and carrot strips and stir again.

2. Place the saucepan over medium heat, cover, and simmer 10 minutes. Uncover and simmer 10 more minutes. Sprinkle with parsley and pepper to serve.

12 servings
Serving size: 1 cup
Starch Exchange...............1
Calories...............................71
Total Fat ....1 g
    Saturated Fat...........0 g
    Calories from Fat 10
Cholesterol ....0 mg
Sodium ....150 mg
Carbohydrate...............15 g
    Dietary Fiber..............3 g
    Sugars ....5 g
Protein ....1 g

Party Black-Eyed Pea Dip

1 15-oz can black-eyed peas, drained and rinsed
1 15 1/2-oz can white hominy, drained and rinsed
1 cup chopped red onion
1 cup chopped green pepper
1/4 cup chopped cilantro or parsley
1 cup salsa
1 4-oz can chopped green chilis
2 medium tomatoes, chopped
2 garlic cloves, minced

1. In a medium bowl, combine all ingredients and mix well. Cover and refrigerate at least 2 hours, stirring occasionally. This allows the flavors to blend and the black-eyed peas and hominy to soften.

2. Remove the dip from the refrigerator and drain. Serve with raw vegetables, whole-wheat crackers, or pita wedges.

23 servings
Serving size: 1/4 cup
Vegetable Exchange...........1
Calories 24
Total Fat..........................0 g
    Saturated Fat...........0 g
    Calories from Fat.........0
Cholesterol ....0 mg
Sodium......................153 mg
Carbohydrate ....5 g
    Dietary Fiber ....1 g
    Sugars ....2 g
Protein ....1 g

Robyn's Split Pea Soup

1 lb dried split green peas
2/3 cup chopped onion
1 cup thinly sliced carrot
1 cup thinly sliced celery
2 cloves garlic, minced
2 sprigs parsley
1 bay leaf
8 cups water
1/2 tsp thyme
1/2 tsp marjoram
1/2 tsp basil
1/2 tsp salt
1/4 tsp cumin
Fresh ground pepper to taste

1. Rinse the split peas thoroughly. Combine all ingredients in a large stockpot and bring to a boil over medium heat.

2. Lower the heat, partially cover the stockpot, and simmer over medium heat for 1 1/2–2 hours until the peas and vegetables are soft. Remove the bay leaf before serving.

8 servings
Serving size: 1 cup
Starch Exchange........2 1/2
Calories............................185
Total Fat ....1 g
   Saturated Fat...........0 g
   Calories from Fat.........9
Cholesterol ....0 mg
Sodium ....156 mg
Carbohydrate...............34 g
   Dietary Fiber.............8 g
   Sugars ....4 g
Protein............................12 g

Lentil Meal in a Pocket

1/4 cup lentils
1/4 cup brown rice
1 1/2 cups water
1/2 cup chopped green onion
1 medium carrot, peeled and shredded
1/2 cup chopped cucumber
1/3 cup low-calorie ranch salad dressing
1 tsp basil
1 tsp parsley
1 clove garlic, minced
2 cups chopped or torn lettuce (1/2-inch pieces)
2 large pita breads, halved and opened into pockets

1. In a small saucepan, combine the lentils, rice, and water. Cook over high heat until boiling, then reduce the heat, cover, and simmer for 20 minutes.

2. Drain the lentils and rice and allow them to cool slightly. Stir in the green onion, carrot, cucumber, ranch dressing, basil, parsley, and garlic.

3. Chill the mixture thoroughly for several hours or overnight. To serve, add the lettuce and spoon the mixture into pita pockets.

4 servings
Serving size: 1 pita pocket
Starch Exchange........2 1/2
Vegetable Exchange...........1
Calories 226
Total Fat ....2 g
   Saturated Fat...........0 g
   Calories from Fat 18
Cholesterol ....0 mg
Sodium.....................357 mg
Carbohydrate...............41 g
   Dietary Fiber..............5 g
   Sugars.........................6 g
Protein ....10 g

Turkey Bean Chili

1 tsp vegetable oil
1 1/2 lb uncooked, boneless, skinless turkey breast, cut into bite-sized pieces
1 cup chopped onion
1 16-oz can black beans, drained and rinsed
1 16-oz can navy beans, drained and rinsed
2 16-oz cans low-fat, low-sodium chicken broth
1 6-oz can no-sodium tomato paste
2 4-oz cans chopped green chilis
1 tsp cumin
1 tsp chili powder

1. In a large stockpot, heat the oil over medium-high heat until hot. Add the turkey and onion and cook until the turkey is no longer pink, about 5–7 minutes.

2. Stir in the remaining ingredients and bring to a boil. Reduce the heat to low. Cook an additional 10–15 minutes, stirring occasionally.

8 servings
Serving size: 1 cup
Starch Exchange.........1 1/2
Lean Meat Exchange.......2
Calories...........................245
Total Fat..........................3 g
    Saturated Fat............1 g
    Calories from Fat.......27
Cholesterol................58 mg
Sodium.....................449 mg
Carbohydrate...............27 g
    Dietary Fiber..............5 g
    Sugars........................6 g
Protein..........................30 g

Tofu Dip with Herbs

12 oz firm tofu, drained and patted dry
1/2 tsp celery seed
1/2 tsp dill
2 Tbsp chopped parsley
1/2 cup diced green onion
1 Tbsp Dijon mustard
1 tsp prepared horseradish
2 medium cloves garlic, pressed
1/2 tsp salt

Process all ingredients in a blender or food processor until very smooth. Serve with fresh vegetables.

6 servings
Serving size: 1/6 recipe
Lean Meat Exchange 1
Calories...........................47
Total Fat ....2 g
    Calories from Fat 18
Cholesterol ....0 mg
Sodium ....216 mg
Carbohydrate.................2 g
    Dietary Fiber ....1 g
Protein ....5 g

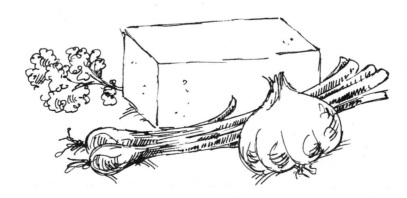

Vegetable Tofu Soup

2 tsp olive or peanut oil
1 1/2 cups chopped onion
3 stalks celery, diagonally sliced
1/2 tsp ginger powder
2 cups sliced mushrooms
1/4 tsp cayenne pepper
1/2 tsp salt
2 bay leaves
4 cups whole tomatoes, chopped (reserve liquid)
1 cup low-fat, low-sodium chicken broth
2 Tbsp tahini
2 Tbsp natural-style peanut butter
12 oz soft tofu, patted dry and cut into 1/2-inch cubes

1. Heat the oil in a large skillet and saute the onion for 5 minutes. Add the celery and ginger and saute for 5 more minutes.

2. Stir in the mushrooms, cover, and simmer for 10 minutes. Add the pepper, salt, and bay leaves. Add the tomatoes with their juice and the chicken broth. Simmer for 20 minutes.

3. Add the tahini and the peanut butter, stirring well to dissolve. Then add the tofu and simmer for another 20 minutes, stirring occasionally.

6 servings
Serving size: 1/6 recipe
Starch Exchange................1
Medium-Fat Meat
    Exchange...........................1
Fat Exchange.......................1
Calories.........................188
Total Fat........................10 g
   Calories from Fat......90
Cholesterol.................0 mg
Sodium....................463 mg
Carbohydrate...............15 g
   Dietary Fiber.............5 g
Protein...............................9 g

Tofu and Spinach Manicotti

2 tsp olive oil
1 medium onion, chopped
3 stalks celery, chopped
3 cloves garlic, crushed
1 Tbsp basil
1 tsp thyme
1 Tbsp oregano
2 15-oz cans no-sodium
   tomato puree
1 cup dry red wine

1 cup water
16 oz soft tofu, drained and
   patted dry
1 10-oz pkg frozen chopped
   spinach, thawed and
   squeezed dry
12 manicotti shells, cooked al
   dente (about 6 oz dry)
1/2 cup grated part-skim
   mozzarella cheese

1. Heat the oil in a large skillet
   and saute the first 6 ingredients over medium heat for 10
   minutes. Add the tomato
   puree, wine, and water. Cover
   and simmer for 25 minutes,
   stirring occasionally.

2. Preheat the oven to 375°F.
   Crumble the tofu and mix it
   well with the spinach. Stuff the
   manicotti shells with the
   mixture. Spread 1 3/4 cups of
   the tomato sauce in a 9 x 13-
   inch baking pan. Place the
   manicotti shells in the sauce
   and cover with the remaining
   sauce.

6 servings
Serving size: 2 shells
Starch Exchange 2
Vegetable Exchange..........2
Medium-Fat Meat
    Exchange 1
Calories 280
Total Fat ....7 g
    Calories from Fat 63
Cholesterol....................5 mg
Sodium ....139 mg
Carbohydrate ....38 g
    Dietary Fiber ....6 g
Protein............................15 g

3. Cover the pan and bake for 45–50 minutes. Sprinkle the
   shells with cheese and bake an additional 5 minutes.

Terrific Tofu

Tofu Burgers

1 Tbsp olive oil
1 large onion, finely chopped
1 large carrot, grated
1 medium green pepper, finely chopped
2 tsp basil
1/2 cup egg substitute
1 1/2 cups seasoned bread crumbs
1/3 cup finely chopped walnuts

1/2 cup chopped parsley
1 Tbsp Dijon mustard
1 Tbsp dark sesame oil
1 Tbsp lite soy sauce (optional)
1/2 tsp pepper
24 oz firm tofu, drained and patted dry

1. Heat the oil in a medium skillet and saute the onion, carrot, green pepper, and basil over medium heat for 10 minutes. In a large bowl, combine the remaining ingredients except the tofu.

2. Mash the tofu with a potato masher and add it to the large bowl. Add the sauted vegetables to the tofu and stir well. Let cool. Preheat the oven to 375°F.

3. Divide the mixture and pat into 6 large patties. Place the patties on a nonstick baking sheet and bake for 30 minutes. Serve on hamburger buns (not included in nutrient analysis).

6 servings
Serving size: 1 patty
Starch Exchange...............1
Vegetable Exchange..........1
Medium-Fat Meat
    Exchange......................2
Fat Exchange.....................1
Calories..........................300
Total Fat.......................15 g
    Calories from Fat.....135
Cholesterol.................0 mg
Sodium....................355 mg
Carbohydrate..............24 g
    Dietary Fiber.............5 g
Protein..........................17 g

Alphabetical List of Recipes

Subject Index

Spicy Lemon-Yogurt Chicken,
171

Desserts (see also Fruit)

Eggplant

Fruit (see also Apples, Berries)

Gazpacho

Lentils

Muffins

Pasta

Pizza

Polenta

Pork

Potatoes

Turkey Gumbo Soup, 65
Vegetable Tofu Soup, 195

Squash

Acorn Squash with Cranberry
Sauce, 124
Apple-Scotch Squash, 169
Curried Hubbard Squash
and Chicken, 167
Posh Squash, 30
Summer Squash Soup, 168

Tofu

Tofu and Spinach Manicotti,
196
Tofu Burgers, 197
Tofu Dip with Herbs, 194
Tofu–Spinach Lasagna, 179
Vegetable Tofu Soup, 195

Tomatoes

Fresh Tomato and Basil Salad,
140
Fresh Tomato Sauce, 45

Turkey

Barbecued Turkey Sandwiches,
67
Individual Savory Turkey
Loaves, 36
Roast Turkey, 117
South-of-the-Border Turkey
Pitas, 64
Spicy Turkey Loaf, 161
Turkey Bean Chili, 193
Turkey Gravy, 118
Turkey Gumbo Soup, 65

Vegetables (see also Eggplant, Potatoes, Rice, Tomatoes)

Candied Yams, 158
Connecticut Mohegan
Succotash, 84
Dhal, 100
Dijon-Style Turnips, 188
Grilled Vegetable Delight, 60
Grilled Vegetable Kabobs, 138
Holiday Snow Peas, 123
Minted Citrus Carrots, 142
Mushrooms Italiano, 104
Parsnip and Carrot
Matchsticks, 189
Red Cabbage, 91
Red Onion Potato Salad, 183
Spicy Greens, 156
Unbeatable Beets, 187

Yogurt

Chilled Yogurt Gazpacho Soup,
170
Spicy Lemon-Yogurt Chicken,
171
Vegetable Salad with Yogurt
Dressing, 127

You'll Get Fabulous New Recipe Ideas and More . . .

Each Month in Diabetes Forecast!

Successful diabetes control is in your hands! *Diabetes Forecast* features exciting, original recipes complete with exchange values.

And there's more! You'll read the latest research news, learn how to avoid complications . . . there's even a children's corner!

Plus, when you subscribe, you become a member of the American Diabetes Association. You'll receive a discount on books, access to the Information Hotline, membership in your local ADA affiliate, and more great benefits in addition to your monthly issue of *Diabetes Forecast*.

Now That's a Recipe for Success!

☐ Yes, I want to join the American Diabetes Association. I've enclosed $24 annual dues.* I will receive 12 issues of *Diabetes Forecast*, membership in my local affiliate, and discounts on all ADA publications.

Name _____

Address _____

City _____ State _____ Zip _____

Telephone _____

Please mail this form with payment to:
American Diabetes Association
General Membership
P.O. Box 363
Mt. Morris, IL 61054–0363

ABK197

*75% of dues is designated for your *Diabetes Forecast* subscription. Allow 6–8 weeks for your first issue of *Diabetes Forecast*. Foreign dues $49. Canadian dues $41.73 (GST included). Mexican dues $39. All dues must be paid in U.S. funds drawn on a U.S. bank. The IRS requires that we inform you that dues are not deductible for Federal income tax purposes.

New Books from the American Diabetes Association Library of Cooking and Self-Care

Flavorful Seasons Cookbook

More than 400 unforgettable recipes that combine great taste with all the good-for-you benefits of a well-balanced meal. Warm up winter with recipes for Christmas, New Year's, St. Patrick's Day, and others. Welcome spring with recipes for Good Friday, Palm Sunday, Easter, Memorial Day, more. Cool off those hot summer days with fresh recipes for the Fourth of July, family barbecues, Labor Day, others. When fall chills the air, you'll be ready with recipes for Halloween, Thanksgiving, and more. #CCBFS
Nonmember: $16.95; ADA Member: $13.55

Diabetic Meals In 30 Minutes—Or Less!

Put an end to bland, time-consuming meals with more than 140 fast, flavorful recipes. Complete nutrition information accompanies every recipe, and a number of "quick tips" will have you out of the kitchen and into the dining room even faster! Here's a quick sample: Salsa Salad, Oven-Baked Parmesan Zucchini, Roasted Red Pepper Soup, and Layered Vanilla Parfait. #CCBDM
Nonmember: $11.95; ADA Member: $9.55

Diabetes Meal Planning Made Easy

The new Diabetes Food Pyramid helps make nutritious meal planning easier than ever. This new guide simplifies the concept by translating diabetes food guidelines into today's food choices. Simple, easy-to-follow chapters will help you understand the new food pyramid; learn all about the six food groups and how to incorporate them into a healthy diet; make smart choices when it comes to sweets, fats, and dairy products; shop smart at the grocery store; make all your meals easier by planning ahead; more. #CCBMP
Nonmember: $14.95; ADA Member: $11.95

Magic Menus for People with Diabetes

Mealtime discipline can be a major struggle—calculating exchanges, counting calories, and figuring fats is complicated and time-consuming. But now you have more than 200 low-fat, calorie-controlled selections—for breakfast, lunch, dinner, and snacks—to automatically turn the struggle into a smorgasbord. Choose from Chicken Cacciatore, Veal Piccata, Chop Suey, Beef Stroganoff, Vegetable Lasagna, plus dozens more. But don't worry about calculating all your nutrients—it's done for you automatically. #CCBMM
Nonmember: $14.95; ADA Member: $11.95

World-Class Diabetic Cooking
Travel around the world at every meal with a collection of 200 exciting new low-fat, low-calorie recipes. Features Thai, Caribbean, Scandinavian, Italian, Greek, Spanish, Chinese, Japanese, African, Mexican, Portuguese, German, and Middle Eastern recipes. All major food categories—appetizers, soups, salads, pastas, meats, breads, and desserts—are highlighted. Includes a nutrient analysis and exchanges (conveniently converted to U.S. exchanges) for each recipe. #CCBWCC
Nonmember: $12.95; ADA Member: $10.35

Southern-Style Diabetic Cooking
Dig into a savory collection of Southern-style recipes without guilt. *Southern-Style Diabetic Cooking* takes traditional Southern dishes and turns them into great-tasting, but good-for-you, recipes. Features more than 100 selections, including appetizers, soups, salads, breads, main dishes, vegetables, side dishes, and desserts. Complete nutrient analysis is included with each recipe, as are suggestions on appropriate frequency of serving and ways to fit special treats or holiday menus into a meal plan. #CCBSSDC
Nonmember: $11.95; ADA Member: $9.55

American Diabetes Association Complete Guide to Diabetes
Finally, all areas of diabetes self-care are covered in the pages of one book. Whether you have type I or type II diabetes, you'll learn all about symptoms and causes, diagnosis and treatment, handling emergencies, complications and prevention, achieving good blood sugar control, and more. You'll also discover advice on nutrition, exercise, sex, pregnancy, travel, family life, coping, and health insurance. 464 pages. Hardcover. Conveniently indexed for quick reference to any topic. #CSMCGD
Nonmember: $29.95; ADA Member: $23.95

How to Get Great Diabetes Care
This book explains the American Diabetes Association's Standards of Care and informs you—step-by-step—of the importance of seeking medical attention that meets these standards. You'll learn about special concerns and treatment options for diabetes-related diseases and conditions. #CSMHGGDC
Nonmember: $11.95; ADA Member: $9.55

Reflections on Diabetes
A collection of stories written by people who have learned from the experience of living with diabetes. Selected from the *Reflections* column of *Diabetes Forecast* magazine, these stories of success, struggle, and pain will inspire you. #CSMROD
Nonmember: $9.95; ADA Member: $7.95

Sweet Kids: How to Balance Diabetes Control and Good Nutrition with Family Peace

At last! A professionally developed collection of advice for parents and caregivers of children with diabetes. Learn all about nutrition and meal planning in diabetes: food, diabetes, and proper development; special areas of concern, such as low blood sugar; self-care techniques for caregivers of children with diabetes; much more. Take advantage of this practical way to educate yourself about how to properly care for a person with diabetes. #CSMSK
Nonmember: $14.95; ADA Member: $11.95

101 Tips for Staying Healthy with Diabetes (and Avoiding Complications)

Developing complications of diabetes is a constant threat without proper self-care. *101 Tips for Staying Healthy* offers the inside track on the latest tips, techniques, and strategies for preventing and treating complications. You'll find simple, practical suggestions for avoiding complications through close blood-sugar control, plus easy-to-follow treatment strategies for slowing and even halting the progression of existing complications. Helpful illustrations with each tip. #CSMFSH
Nonmember: $12.50; ADA Member: $9.95

Bestsellers

Diabetes A to Z

In clear, simple terms, you'll learn all about blood sugar, complications, diet, exercise, heart disease, insulin, kidney disease, meal planning, pregnancy, sex, weight loss, and much more. Alphabetized for quick reference. #CGFDAZ
Nonmember: $9.95; ADA Member: $7.95

Managing Diabetes on a Budget

For less than $10 you can begin saving hundreds and hundreds on your diabetes self-care. An inexpensive, surefire collection of "do-it-this-way" tips and hints to save you money on everything from medications and diet to exercise and health care. #CSMMDOAB
Nonmember: $7.95; ADA Member: $6.25

The Fitness Book: For People with Diabetes

You'll learn how to exercise to lose weight, exercise safely, increase your competitive edge, get your mind and body ready to exercise, much more. #CSMFB
Nonmember $18.95; ADA Member: $14.95

Raising a Child with Diabetes

Learn how to help your child adjust insulin to allow for foods kids like to eat, have a busy schedule and still feel healthy and strong, negotiate the twists and turns of being "different," accept the physical and emotional challenges life has to offer, and much more. #CSMRACWD
Nonmember: $14.95; ADA Member: $11.95

The Dinosaur Tamer

Enjoy 25 fictional stories that will entertain, enlighten, and ease your child's frustrations about having diabetes. Each tale warmly evaporates the fear of insulin shots, blood tests, going to diabetes camp, and more. Ages 8–12. #CSMDTAOS
Nonmember: $9.95; ADA Member: $7.95

101 Tips for Improving Your Blood Sugar

101 Tips offers a practical, easy-to-follow roadmap to tight blood sugar control. One question appears on each page, with the answers or "tips" below each question. Tips on diet, exercise, travel, weight loss, insulin injection, illness, sex, and much more.
#CSMTBBGC
Nonmember: $12.50; ADA Member $9.95

Order Toll-Free! 1-800-ADA-ORDER (232-6733)
VISA • MasterCard • American Express

Or send your check or money order to:
American Diabetes Association
ATTN: Order Fulfillment Department
P.O. Box 930850
Atlanta, GA 31193–0850

Shipping & Handling

Up to $30..add $3.00
$30.01–$50 ....add $4.00
Above $50 ....add 8% of order

Allow 2–3 weeks for shipment. Add $3 to shipping & handling for each extra shipping address. Add $15 for each overseas shipment. Prices subject to change without notice.

Also available in bookstores nationwide